The POWER Series

DESERT RATS

The British 4 and 7 Armoured Brigades

Hans Halberstadt

Motorbooks International
Publishers & Wholesalers ®

For Major General and Mrs. P.A.J. Cordingley,
with a salute and thanks.

First published in 1993 by Motorbooks International Publishers & Wholesalers, PO Box 2, 729 Prospect Avenue, Osceola, WI 54020 USA

Motorbooks International is a certified trademark, registered with the United States Patent Office

The information in this book is true and complete to the best of our knowledge. All recommendations are made without any guarantee on the part of the author or Publisher, who also disclaim any liability incurred in connection with the use of this data or specific details

We recognize that some words, model names and designations, for example, mentioned herein are the property of the trademark holder. We use them for identification purposes only. This is not an official publication

Motorbooks International books are also available at discounts in bulk quantity for industrial or sales-promotional use. For details write to Special Sales Manager at the Publisher's address

Library of Congress Cataloging-in-Publication Data
Halberstadt, Hans.
    Desert rats / Hans Halberstadt.
       p. cm.—(The Power series)
    Includes index.
    ISBN 0-87938-767-X
    1. Great Britain. Army. Armoured Brigade, 4th.
2. Great Britain. Army. Armoured Brigade, 7th.
I. Title.   II. Series: Power series (Osceola, Wis.)
UA655 4th.H35   1993
358′.1830941—dc20   93-13161

On the front cover: The British Army is deeply rooted in traditions, which are carried with the individual regiments wherever they go. This pipe-and-drum corps is with the Royal Scots Dragoon Guards. *Bob Morrison/Military Scene*

On the back cover: Top, a British Chieftain tank on maneuvers in Germany. *Will Fowler.* A mounted Guards Regiment soldier on post near Whitehall in London.

On the title page: The British Army's new tank, the Challenger 2, designed by Vickers Defence Systems. *Vickers*

On the frontispiece: A modern Desert Rat.

Printed and bound in Hong Kong

Contents

Acknowledgments

I'm especially grateful for the support of two British Army officers for their support and assistance in the development of this portrait, Major General Patrick Cordingley and Major Will Fowler. The general's enthusiastic interest and hospitality while commander of the Combined Arms Training Centre made my research visit to the United Kingdom a delight. With his sponsorship, I was able to get insights into this society that I could never have obtained otherwise.

I am likewise indebted to Major Fowler for the same kinds of insights and hospitality. Major Fowler had one of the most dangerous, disgusting, dreaded jobs of any member of the British armed forces during the war in the Gulf—babysitting journalists. Despite this, Will took on another "journo," and managed to keep him from getting into too much trouble.

The Combined Arms Training Centre in Warminster provided a large cast of characters who contributed to this story: besides the general, I should thank Majors Baxter Innes, Gillespie, and Martin McKane-Brunner; Warrant Officer 2 "Rooster" Barber; plus a large number of supporting players too numerous to mention. It was a real treat to watch the centre train British soldiers with a level of realistic hazard that is, unfortunately, seldom found in American programs.

And, a salute to Brigadier Tim Glass and Major Kate Martin of the Department of Public Relations for the British Army. The British Army has a rather more protective policy about the production of such projects as this one than the US Army does, but consented to support the book anyway.

Preface

From an American perspective—which is definitely the point of view of this book—the little congregation called the British Army is a fascinating, glittering thing, quite unlike the comparatively faceless, endless ranks of US Army forces. As a product of the US Army, I am a fond admirer of its many talents and virtues. I've worked extensively with (and, as far as that goes, recruited) the US Army's Rangers, "Green Berets," Airborne, plus some of the best light infantry and armor units. I've also studied and worked with our own marvelous Marine Corps, Navy, and Air Force, and the professionalism of the people and the excellence of their equipment and doctrine are all superb. But after visiting British forces in England and meeting some of the officers and men who fought so well in the Iraqi desert I came away thinking how dull and drab and really *boring* we Americans are. That, and how much we have to learn from these remarkable people and their terrific little army.

We need to learn from them because our army will soon be smaller, too—much smaller than when we expected to keep the world safe for freedom and democracy. The armies that beat Iraq have been defeated by the budget committees that fund them. Britain's small force has

FIBUA ("fighting in built-up areas") training at the Combined Arms Training Centre, Warminster, Wiltshire, is nearly as dangerous, challenging and exhausting as the genuine article.

succeeded somehow in developing and maintaining an army that has demonstrated vividly it can do what it was hired to do: to deploy long distances on short notice, to fight under the worst of conditions, to prevail against the nations' enemies. What we Americans have been able to do with sheer weight-of-arms the British manage to accomplish largely with a smaller, better trained corps of officers and soldiers.

Now, I know better than most people how well we train our people and how good our weapons are. But the British Army has some advantages over ours that are worth study and emulation, particularly in these difficult times for American military communities. These advantages are a mixed bag, starting with extremely high standards for soldiers and leaders. As an example, we train people for three fairly gentle weeks and pin paratrooper wings on them; the Brits make their program six months long—and it is brutal. One instructor at the Basic Airborne School at Fort Benning, Georgia, told me that the training schedule for the program was designed to appeal to the trainees' mothers, and I concur. Anybody in reasonable health can become an American "jump-qualified" soldier today, but very few of these men and women are qualified to jump into a combat zone without a lot more training. The British program is far more realistic and appropriate—and despite far higher standards of admission, it has a far higher failure rate. And that's the kind of lesson we need to apply to our own training.

Who Are the Desert Rats?

The expression "Desert Rat" was born in 1938 among the very ratty British forces opposing aggressive Italian activity in North Africa. It was applied to the British 7 Armoured Division when it was formed in 1940—then to all of the huge British 8 Army—and preserved informally after the war by 4 and 7 Armoured Brigades, the major remnants of that once immense corps.

When Iraq invaded Kuwait in August of 1990, Brigadier Patrick Cordingley's 7 Armoured Brigade, a tank-heavy force, was the logical British contribution to the Coalition of forces assembled to defend Saudi Arabia. The 4 Brigade followed, along with a large contingent of British units, active and reserve. They all thought of themselves as lawful heirs of the old North African Rats, and since they came from across the whole of the British Army, the honor belongs to them all.

So this book is a portrait of more than just the specific units that fought (and fueled and fed) in the Gulf, but the whole institution that put them there. It is about their heritage, manners, morals, weapons, language, mission, and training. It is also about what they did in the Gulf, and how it happened.

This Army has been held in some contempt by British civilians ever since Oliver Cromwell's never-forgotten ten years of direct military gov-

A MILAN anti-tank missile section in Gulf. Milan is a proven anti-tank missile similar to the US tube-launched, optically-tracked, wire guided (TOW) missile. Will Fowler

The fabled little red rat, the insignia of 7 Armoured Brigade, is actually rather brown. The insignia has been used since 1938 when a small, ill-equipped British mobile force was assigned to secure the vital Suez Canal from Italian forces threatening from the west. Legend has it that the rat was inspired by a soldier's pet Jerboa, a little rodent native to the harsh desert, and was adopted by the units that ultimately became the British 7 Armoured Division.

ernment in the 1650s, which has forced the institution to manufacture its own society, something it has done enthusiastically. It insulated and isolated itself from the larger society and culture that it guards, by mutual consent. There is nothing unusual about that. The same thing happens in Russia, America, and just about anywhere else, by mutual consent of the two alien cultures, civil and military. Being part of any army is a kind of calling, like religious service, that makes you different in almost every external and internal way.

Unlike the American pattern, British units are each highly unique communities with their own attire, traditions, language, and style. They've been called "tribes"—an excellent analogy. For the most part, these tribes currently cooperate, at least in the face of a national enemy. Although, on Friday nights the enemy can be anybody from a different regiment.

The foundation for this army is the British Army regiment, an institution as strong, durable, and essential as the monarchy. And if the members of the different regiments like to brawl with each other, that's part of the ancient tradition, too. Modern England, despite the civilized veneer and compact size (about the size of the state of California) retains many cultural elements of ancient tribal times, and those cultures still echo within British society and most loudly within the army. The regiments of today's army are the clear descendants of the bands of Celts, Saxons, Welshmen, and Irish who fought each other in the past and were gradually hammered together into a kind of social and military amalgam that we call Great Britain. It makes a strong combination, and a handsome one too because you can still see the individual components within the pattern of the whole. In fact the regimental tradition is so strong that many attempts to dispose of it have failed; it seems likely to survive into the foreseeable future.

Those tribal components have good tribal names, so unlike their faceless American counterparts: The Staffordshire Regiment (The Prince of Wales'), The Royal Scots Dragoon Guards (Carabiniers & Greys), The Queen's

The black rat is the 4 Armoured Brigade insignia in a slightly altered posture. The old 7 Armoured Division of World War II included both 7 Brigade and 4 Brigade; when 4 Brigade was later reassigned, after the capture of Tunis, they wished to retain the little Jerboa as their emblem, but had to do so in an altered form. The black rat was the result.

Private Shanahan is participating in some extremely challenging training in combat in urban environments at the excellent Combined Arms Training Centre, Wiltshire, on the Salisbury Plain near Stonehenge.

Royal Irish Hussars, The King's Own Scottish Borderers, The Royal Highland Fusiliers, 16/5 The Queen's Royal Lancers. The difference between these units and others within the British Army is more than the cosmetics of an elaborate name. Uniforms can be different, particularly the beret, even when the soldiers aren't wearing their dress uniforms or ceremonial attire, and regimental formal uniforms are tremendously diverse. Even the language spoken in one unit will differ greatly from that in another. While at the School of Infantry at Warminster, out on Salisbury Plain in the west of England, I overheard two young tankers from the Royal Scots Dragoon Guards chattering away about some business or other. With nothing else to do, I

A Gulf War veteran member of the Household Cavalry Guards Horse Guards, the London Military District headquarters. In the Gulf he would have crewed an armored vehicle. The British Army, unlike the American, combined ceremonial and tactical responsibilities for some select units.

listened to them for some minutes—and didn't understand a *single* word. Despite the fact that these two were almost within arms' reach and were conversing enthusiastically, I could not understand them. They and I both speak English (or think we do), but their heavy Scottish dialect (which is beautiful, musical, and easy to understand with a little practice) is not the same language we use at home in California—or that spoken in London, for that matter, or in Wales either. Even within the compact spaces of the British Isles these little tribes survive, even today, in and out of the army. That difference would not be tolerated, much less celebrated, in the military communities across the Atlantic in America—a country that publicly promotes diversity. Well, diversity is the name of the game in the British Army.

If the American model were employed by British personnel officers, recruits from all parts of the nation would be assigned to units with recruits from everywhere else. During the course of a career a soldier may serve with many different units—the 24th Infantry, the 82nd Airborne, the 1st Armored Division, the 7th Infantry Division (Light); members of the units will come and go constantly, off to other assignments and new homes. That's not how it works with the Brits. Instead, as was once the case in the United States, recruiting for units is normally done within a localized geographic area. Regiments have a "home" county, usually, and once assigned to such a regiment a soldier can expect to stay with the same faces until they're all old, scarred, and wrinkled.

As a result, British Army units are tight little families. Like families anywhere, not everybody likes everybody else in the family—and sometimes one family will enjoy brawling with its neighbors. Also like other families, rituals and ceremonies bind people together and celebrate strengths and traditions. I admire these tribal rituals—they provide a strength for the force and for the people who serve in them. They are a refuge, and more. Some American military communities incorporate elements of this sense of tradition and heritage, too, like the US Marine Corps, which uses the regimental system and

A Kevin Lyles drawing for 1 Battalion, Royal Scots' *version of the Desert Rat badge.* Kevin Lyles

Captain Hutton of the Queen's Royal Irish Hussars wears the distinctive beret insignia of his regiment. Officers in the British Army frequently come from the upper classes, unlike in the US Army; it is still a respected profession in the United Kingdom where the profession of arms still attracts the best and the brightest of British society.

has a sense of self with all the swagger and starch of any regiment of guards.

War and warriors are a fascinating subject, for many reasons. The stresses of mortal combat have an interesting way of cutting to the truth about people and societies. In this business, the most primitive human qualities of raw, brazen courage, endurance of pain, of commitment and friendship, and wisdom under the most stressful circumstances win battles and change history. The "Paras" showed this on their epic march in the Falklands, just as the first generation of Desert Rats did outside Alexandria in 1940; we call it *gallantry*, and it is a rare thing. But the flip side of the issue deals with the tools of the trade—equally important when you are trying to carve history. Raw courage can make up for a lot, but the line between courage and foolish sacrifice is a fine one; it takes courage and good weapons to fight successfully.

Weaponry brings up another interesting part of the modern Desert Rats' story. Britain has combined leading-edge technology with tradi-

tional military values to produce its force for many centuries, and does so today. The "Chobham" laminate armor on British tanks is one example of this commitment to technological superiority; it is probably the most bullet-resistant material anywhere. When a British tanker fired at an Iraqi main battle tank, as an experiment, over five kilometers away—far beyond the published maximum effective range of the weapon—and destroyed it with the first round, he demonstrated another kind of battlefield superiority that shapes history.

So the British Army that went off to the desert in 1990 was a curious, charming, fascinating congregation of extremely diverse people, ancient and usually honorable traditions, the most modern weapons, and the most fundamental of battle skills—new and old, primitive and complex, plain and fancy, young recruits and old generals, individuals and clans—the little army that does big things, the Desert Rats.

The Saga of the Desert Rat in World War II

What they say about North Africa isn't true—that business about it being a trackless waste, with sun-blasted sand as far as the eye can see. No, North Africa is actually a land of four seasons and considerable variety to entertain the tourist. At times, of course, it is incredibly hot and dry with temperatures well over 130 degrees Fahrenheit for days on end—so hot that movement seems not only impossible but irrational. But, the nights of those same days can be down in the fifties . . . chill enough to need a coat or sweater to be comfortable. And while the place is indeed sandy, it is not invariably dry; in fact the proximity of the Mediterranean Sea to the north means the climate of North Africa is often damp as well as hot or cold. One can easily be standing in a sodden foxhole, up to the knees in muddy water, with sand blowing in the eyes. The sand blows all the time thanks to a wind that reliably circulates the heat (or cold) without moderating it. With no trees to break its flow, the wind can blast down across the desert with considerable force, abrading everything in its path.

So North Africa is a region full of climatic variety, with miserable heat, miserable cold,

The Gordon Highlanders, led by their piper and a subaltern wearing the Glengarry slog across the border into Tunisia during the final advance of the North African campaign during World War II. Imperial War Museum

appalling humidity, and desiccating dryness–all of which are sometimes available for the tourist on the same day. And that business about the endless sand dunes is likewise exaggerated; there are, indeed, miles of treacherous sand dunes, but North Africa is a land of contrasts, with miles of lunar rock fields, arid hills devoid of vegetation, deep wadis, rocky escarpments, and bare mountains, too. Occasionally, for variety, a small oasis with a few palm trees and a mud house or two pops up. Along the very edge of the coast are a few miles of land suitable for agriculture, with groves of citrus and olive trees, and sometimes grapes, but so little as to be almost unnoticeable. Inland the trees disappear quickly, turning to scrub bushes and sparse grass.

A rich variety of wildlife calls North Africa home. Flies by the zillion await the passing visitor, and fleas are always ready for breakfast, as well as scorpions and occasional snakes. Human beings will wander through from time to time, usually as quickly as their transportation will permit. And some of them have instincts to match the rest of the fauna in the neighborhood.

While most animal life in North Africa has long since gone elsewhere in search of a happy home, one small creature survives here and manages to prosper. It is a little rodent called the *Jerboa* by technicians, the "desert rat" by everybody else. It's a cheerful and industrious critter that has managed to adapt to the desert and find enough resources to thrive, even here. It digs below the surface to avoid heat and enemies, scavenges far and wide for food, and remains alert to its enemies, the patrolling hawks and snakes that pounce on the occasional rat whose tactics are unsound.

The little desert rat was left pretty much unmolested by humanity until 1938 when a new pestilence of the worst kind was visited on North Africa—the Italian Army.

Now, the Italian Army of the 1930s had just about everything a modern military force of the time required: millions of men, lots of modern small arms, excellent support aircraft, artillery, transport, cute uniforms, superb (for an army) food, a big budget, and even a supply of *vino* to keep the troops relaxed. Unfortunately, it was staffed almost entirely by Italians—marvelous people, without a doubt, but just not warrior material ever since Augustus Caesar retired as commander-in-chief some years earlier.

Despite this handicap, the Fascist government headed by Benito Mussolini shipped the Italian Army off to Africa (through the Suez canal, with British consent) to start accumulating a new Italian empire in October of 1935. Without any real pretext, this force attacked the ancient, feudal, primitive kingdom of Ethiopia. The Ethiopians, armed with spears, courage, and audacity, gave the Italians a few rough moments before being annihilated by the aircraft, infantry, and light armor of the invaders. It took a quarter of a million Italians, using

The appearance of British troops scattered overseas at the beginning of World War II reflected their previous role as Imperial Garrisons rather than the realities of the battles to come. Here men of the South Stafford-shire Regiment—whose lineal descendants were to fight in the Gulf fifty years later—march out from their camp at Helouan, Egypt, in June 1940. Imperial War Museum

modern weapons and poison gas, six months to win the sad little war. The world community looked on and—despite the grand promises of the League of Nations at the conclusion of the "war to end all wars"—did nothing.

For the world's only real super power of the time, the empire of Great Britain, Italy's actions were cause for real alarm. Although not to the same degree as the United States, the British had substantially reduced their military forces following World War I as an economic measure, and despite the renewed threat from Germany and Japan, were slow to respond.

But the threat to the Empire was real, obvious, and profoundly dangerous. Italy had developed a modern, heavy naval force after World War I and was now threatening to use it. For the Brits, with an empire sprinkled throughout the world and rather lightly defended, the Italian threat was a problem. And the key to the problem—a veritable linchpin—was the canal at Suez, connecting the Mediterranean to the Red Sea, connecting England to India, Singapore, Hong Kong, Burma, Malaya, Kenya, and all of Arabia. If the Italians, with their ships, tanks, and airplanes, could take Ethiopia, then perhaps they could take Suez. And if they took Suez, the entire empire would be in peril.

The preliminaries for World War II took place during the next few years in Spain, China, and Europe, much to the horror of the United States and England where memories of World War I were fresh and pacifist feelings were strong.

As a result, the little *Jerboa* got some company out in the desert west of Alexandria, Egypt, in 1938—some ragged battalions of what was supposed to be armor, some artillery batteries with virtually useless guns, and a few hundred British infantrymen. The tanks were obsolete, based on standards from the great unpleasantness of twenty years before, as were the guns, and a lot of the soldiers. Some of the armored scout cars were actually left over from the First World War. The tanks, newer but built to already obsolete standards, traveled on tracks that were nearly worn out. There was no ammunition at all for the heavy machine guns. There were few heavy trucks for transport. Food and ammuni-

Among the most obnoxious of the fates and fortunes of war in the desert were the flies—tiny, ever-present, and maddening. Imperial War Museum

Italian prisoners bring their wounded to a British ambulance after a battle. Imperial War Museum

17

tion for the soldiers were sparse. And the number of soldiers was pathetically small, even counting the new arrivals who were untrained or not acclimatized.

Training and reconnaissance began immediately. Number 11 Hussars (pronounced *hus-SARs*) prowled hundreds of miles to the west, developing a detailed map of the terrain and its ability to support tanks and trucks. Aggressive training and planning commenced with whatever resources were available. Ancient and obsolete tanks, trucks, and light armored scout cars were supplemented with newer ones. All were serviced by an efficient system of careful inspec-

tion and maintenance before being committed to units in the field.

The soldiers themselves rapidly adapted to the conditions of the desert. Uniform standards became exceedingly casual. So did the standards for military courtesies like saluting, particularly when soldiers from the many Commonwealth nations encountered each other back in Cairo where senior officers on the street might be informed by cocky Australians that "We ain't salutin' today, mate."

Units from around the empire gradually arrived from Australia, Rhodesia, and South Africa. They learned to survive on a gallon of water

The US-made M3 Grant tank gave the British armored regiments improved firepower and a reliable engine but its tall profile and the low position of the 75mm sponson gun—for which ammo is being loaded here—*made it difficult to adopt hull-down firing positions, with often fatal consequences.* Imperial War Museum

a day, for drinking, cooking, bathing, and washing; later they'd learn to do it on a half-gallon. They ate well, though—if you like rice and jam three times a day, at a half-pound of each for days on end. Later it would be canned beef three times a day, sometimes enlivened with captured Italian tomato paste. They all learned to survive the *Khamseen*, a searing wind that comes up from the Sahara to the south, raising huge clouds of stinging dust. When the wind blew, life on the desert essentially stopped—eating, drinking, sleeping, and fighting were all virtually impossible. It was not always a lot of fun.

British soldiers have a long tradition of adaptation to stress and deprivation, normally by the application of large quantities of humor and strong tea. There are two versions of the genesis of the desert rat name; the first holds that, around 1938, the members of the force opposing the Italian Army in the desert noticed the little desert rat and its industry and apparent cheerful demeanor. It was not long before they started referring to themselves as desert rats. The other credits the German propaganda radio broadcasts by the traitor "Lord Haw-Haw" for the name, a sneering reference to the besieged defenders of Tobruk in 1941. The sneer backfired, according to this version, when the entire 8 Army started referring to themselves as desert rats.

Training continued in traditional British style. In late spring of 1940, the force that would later become 7 Armoured Division was conducting maneuvers on the desert near Gerawla—a "mechanized hunt meeting" they called it, as if it were a fox hunt at home.

Bookies took bets on the entrants, and a lance corporal dressed in "drag" to play the part of the Duchess of Gerawla, bestowing prizes on successful riders of their metal "steeds." During this playful training exercise a radio message arrived: France had fallen. Italy had entered the war.

Facing the Rats across the wire and fortifications of the western Egyptian frontier in early June of 1940 was a vast army of fourteen Italian divisions and approximately 215,000 men. This huge force was deployed in Libya, facing British

Infantry from the fabled Black Watch charge into battle aboard a little Valentine tank on 1 April 1943. Imperial War Museum

Egypt, and being constantly supplied from bases just across the Mediterranean Sea.

Opposing them were about 20,000 British soldiers, and only part of them available for combat. They were the ragged members of 7 Armoured Division, a detached infantry brigade and two freshly arrived, untrained and unequipped Commonwealth divisions not suitable for combat. Even 7 Armoured was not fully prepared for combat operations, some units still lacked training, tanks, artillery, and ammunition. All of this was commanded by General Sir Archibald Wavell, Commander-in-Chief Middle East.

World War II in the Desert Begins

At one in the morning of 11 June 1940, the British Empire declared war on Italy, and the desert force went immediately into action. Number 11 Hussars cut the wire dividing the Italian force to the west from the British forces and went off in search of adventure—and some more tomato paste. Within days this force captured several hundred prisoners at small cost and

Wounded British soldiers from the 51 Highland Division are collected at a casualty point after an engagement with the Afrikakorps at El Alamein, October 1942. Imperial War Museum

destroyed a fair number of enemy tanks and trucks. On the fourteenth an Italian fort was captured by 7 Hussars, and another fort surrendered after a bombing raid.

On the sixteenth, the first armor engagement took place when twelve Italian tanks and thirty trucks were destroyed by a task force from 7 and 11 Hussars with support from the Royal Horse Artillery. Two entire companies of Italian tanks plus a motorized artillery battery—an entire battalion—were wiped out at a cost to the Brits of not a single soldier killed or wounded.

The Italian commander, Marshall Rodolfo Graziani, prepared a counterattack against the massive army he assumed was facing him and attacked on 13 September 1940. The Italian attack was massive, and incompetent. Thirty-five hundred Italians became casualties at a cost of 150 Rats. The crucial British position at the little town of Mersa Matruh was ignored by the enemy. Although pressed by the sheer numbers of the enemy, and occasionally challenged by the isolated competence of enemy commanders and the genuine bravery of individual enemy soldiers, the major tactical problem for the Rats was coming up with enough ammunition to kill the Italians blundering around out in the kill zones and finding enough food to feed the prisoners of war (POWs) who were surrendering in multitudes.

"Jock Columns" and the Development of Combined Arms Teams

The commander of 4 Royal Horse Artillery, Lt. Col. J. C. Campbell, started assembling and launching into combat little "jock columns," which we call "combined arms teams" or "task forces" today. These are task-organized, temporary units with infantry, artillery, and armor units included, each with talents and resources and liabilities. If properly designed and used, these little combat teams (typically about company- or battalion-sized) can be remarkably effective as an independent force, a sum much greater than its conventional component parts.

Despite a fairly extreme imbalance of forces, the Rats rather quickly consumed the enemy army. British doctrine was innovative, imaginative, and encouraged energy and initiative, while Italian doctrine was the reverse. The Brits used the desert like the surface of a large sea and fought a battle of movement on it. The Desert Rats applied naval rules of maneuver to the battle, and large numbers of Italian tanks, trucks, and infantry were wrecked against the rocky shoals of the western desert, out-generaled and out-soldiered at every turn. The little task forces—approximately battalion strength —were defeating entire brigades and sometimes nearly entire divisions. Nineteen forty might have been a bleak year for the allies in many ways but not in North Africa where Wavell's Army of the Nile was offering at least one bright glimmer of hope.

The battle had begun in September, with Italian forces already in Egypt, only about 200 miles west of Alexandria on the Mediterranean coast in relatively small encounters. But by December the Brits had built up the force so it could do some serious fighting, and the rout was on. During December and into January of 1941 the little Rats took half the Italian Army out of the war through the death or capture of 125,000 Italian soldiers and pushed the remnants back 500 miles into Libya.

The German general Erwin Rommel arrived in Tripoli in February with an armored corps and supporting aviation units to back up the Italians. While nominally under Italian command, Rommel and his staff quickly took over the war in the desert—from the British as well as the Italians.

Rommel launched a counteroffensive on 24 March against a Rat-pack that had been spread thin by the vast distances, large numbers of POWs, and by the reassignment of much of Wavell's force to Greece. Quite suddenly the Army of the Nile was making a run for it. Within a space of two weeks nearly all the territory the Italians had lost had been regained—plus about a hundred and fifty miles of former British territory. German tanks were seventy miles west of Alexandria. All the Libyan coastline was secure—except for the little port city called Tobruk.

The Germans were a different enemy for the Rats, with vastly superior guns, tanks, and tactical procedures. German planes based in Sicily and Tripolitania quickly mined the Suez canal. When they weren't dropping mines they dropped bombs or strafed ground targets. And they supported Rommel's forces who were attempting to reduce the little Tobruk garrison that refused to crack. The Tobruk enclave distracted Rommel from completing his victory and was a dangerous threat on his left flank.

The Empire Strikes Back

General Sir Archibald Wavell was relieved by General Sir Claude Auchinleck in June. The Rats were now the 8 Army, and they fought back as best they could. The Germans were out at the end of a very long and weak supply line, and the Brits found theirs suddenly a bit shorter than before. The forces were essentially equal, the battles sparring contests between matched contenders, with one round going to the Axis,

The M3 Grant tank, with its seven-man crew, was wasteful of manpower—terminally so if the tank were hit and "brewed up." Imperial War Museum

another to the Rats. It went like that for fourteen months. Then Tobruk fell.

Auchinleck was replaced by General Sir Harold Alexander. An obscure little general was selected to command 8 Army; the new commander was Lieutenant General Bernard Law Montgomery. "Monty" was an odd man—fifty-five at the time, physically small, strong-willed, detested by much of the British officer corps, bull-headed, and often rude. He was also formidably intelligent. While some in London criticized his seeming lack of aggressiveness, those closer to him saw a commitment to get it *right* this time.

He roamed the entire 8 Army, speaking to soldiers, seeing and being seen. While other commanders had stayed in their headquarters, plotting and scheming with the staff, Montgomery put on an old black beret he'd been given by the Royal Tank Regiment and went visiting. He added his general's badge to the Royal Tank Regiment insignia, offending some officers but delighting the rank and file; until then British generals simply didn't wear personal uniforms.

As sometimes happens in war, an obscure man rises to the occasion and works miracles. Rommel and Montgomery were both such men. Monty reenergized the Army of the Nile just as Rommel had done for the Axis side—but unlike Rommel, he did it slowly, methodically, and with maddening attention to detail. In the process of building his force, he antagonized and alienated many, both in England and in North Africa, who wanted the same swift stroke that Rommel had used so successfully.

Whatever Monty's faults, he and the Desert Rats beat Rommel, and in war, winning excuses almost everything. It took a while and it was never a sure thing until very late in the game. It began just as Rommel was about to pounce on the defeated British Commonwealth forces just sixty miles outside Alexandria, Egypt, in 1942, at a nasty bit of ground called El Alamein.

El Alamein was the Axis high watermark. Just as the victory medals were being minted in Germany, as Mussolini was sending his favorite white horse across the Mediterranean for use in the imminent victory parade planned for Cairo,

and the Afrikakorps and Italian Army were preparing to pounce, Montgomery's Desert Rats attacked. The ground they chose was a narrow channel of passable ground; on the south was the impassable Quattara Depression, a crusted sand trap that prevented any kind of movement. On the north lay the Mediterranean. In between were mines, tanks, guns, and infantry—facing each other across a narrow, forty-mile front . . . and waiting.

The attack kicked off on 23 October 1942, a bright, moon-lit evening, while Rommel reported to Hitler and the German High Command back in Germany. Sappers went first, clearing lanes through the mine fields, and the Rats assaulted to the west. Every available artillery tube—a thousand guns—pumped steel down range, sheltering the attack with fire. Mortars fired illumination rounds over enemy positions, revealing targets for the tanks and troops moving forward. A thousand guns fired for five hours.

Montgomery might have been slow and methodical, but when the Rats attacked it was with a force that out-numbered and out-gunned the

Sherman tanks of C Squadron, 9 Lancers, 1 Armoured Division sweep across a stretch of open desert that recalls the frequent comparison of the tank battles of *North Africa to naval campaigns.* Imperial War Museum

Axis opposition two-to-one. And the 8 Army had Rats from Scotland, Wales, New Zealand, Australia, India—black Africans and pasty Britons—all ready to get on with it. Montgomery had trained them, inspired them, given them the tools to win, and finally turned them loose on the enemy as an avenging host out of Egypt.

The Axis forces had become over extended, out at the end of a tenuous supply line; even so, Rommel risked a trip back to Germany. With Montgomery's plodding caution, with fourteen months of experience and victories, with Alexandria only sixty miles away, victory for the Afrikakorps should have been guaranteed. But

The British up-gunned the Sherman during 1943 by fitting their long-barrel 17-pounder antitank gun to the turret. This "Firefly" variant, usually issued at the rate of one per troop, gave them a weapon capable of killing the German Tiger tank. One of the crewmen loading the big 17-pounder shells here wears a favorite affectation of the World War II "Tommy," a leather trouser belt decorated with traded cap badges from regiments serving alongside his unit. Imperial War Museum

A military policeman directs traffic near Tunis, Tunisia, in April of 1943. Crown Copyright

it wasn't. The attack's ferocity, when it came, was stunning, stupefying in its violence, its noise, its confusion. There was no stopping the British who surged out across the front, behind a rolling artillery barrage, sucking up the Axis units battalion by battalion.

The German commander in Rommel's absence, General Georg von Stumme, dropped dead of a heart attack. Thousands of other German and Italian soldiers dropped dead—of wounds from .303-caliber Lee Enfield rifles, three-inch heavy mortar rounds, twenty-five-pound artillery, and tank main guns. It took two days for Rommel to return; when he did, it was to a transformed Afrikakorps, much of which was now in smoldering ruin.

Hitler ordered Rommel to stand fast, to win or to die in place. It was the order of a lunatic. Rommel obeyed it for a few days, watched his force being uselessly consumed, and then pulled back from the furnace of El Alamein. The retreat was a fighting withdrawal, not a rout, that took the Afrikakorps all the way to Tunisia across

1,700 miles during the next eighty days. And at the end of the march were fresh supplies, new tanks, more men, and ammunition that survived the perilous passage across the Mediterranean from Italy. Along the way the Rats fought the Axis at Tobruk on 13 November, Benghazi on the twentieth, El Agheila and Merduma from late November till early December, Buerat el Hsur in Tripolitania for another two weeks, and again at Tripoli on 23 January.

For the retreating Germans and Italians it must have been a gloomy march. On November 8, Allied forces executed Operation Torch, the invasion of French Morocco and Algeria. The prospect of victory or even survival, so tangible only weeks before, slid from view for Rommel and the survivors. But Rommel wasn't called the Desert Fox for being foolish. Despite being caught in the biggest pincer movement in military history, the Afrikakorps and its foxy leader consumed many Rats before one last campaign on the battlefields around Tunis. In mid-February, near the Tunisian town of Kasserine, the US II Corps was badly beaten, and 2,500 Americans were captured. II Corps was thrown back through the Kasserine Pass in confusion and its units were slaughtered by German armor, artillery, and aviation; it was a costly lesson for the Americans, but well learned.

Rommel was extracted from Africa in March as defeat became inevitable. With the Brits attacking from the east and the British 1 Army and the American II Corps coming in from the west, one key terrain feature after another was lost to the remnants of the Afrikakorps and the surviving Italians. Tunis fell on 7 May. Italy and Germany had lost a third of a million men in the struggle, and with them any hope for victory. About seven hundred Germans escaped before the garrison finally fell on 13 May 1943.

Montgomery and the British 8 Army went on after the survivors, into Italy where most of the divisions spent the rest of the war. Number 7 Armoured Division was pulled out of Italy to participate in the Normandy invasion and fought on all the way to Berlin and Allied victory in May 1945. When the shooting finally stopped, six long, hard years had passed and with them passed many Desert Rats, killed or wounded. In fact, nearly none of the British soldiers who met the Italians in the desert west of Alexandria in 1939 would escape the fates and fortunes of war until VE-day in May of 1945; virtually all the units had suffered about 100 percent casualties by then.

Stand Down for the British Army

It would be nice to report that the legendary 8 Army and its constituent units lived on into the present, but it didn't quite work out that way. After the war, England disbanded and abolished many fine old units of long service. Numbers 4 and 7 Armoured Divisions had been brigades early in the conflict, and brigades they became

again, although without the clear lineage of legitimate descendants.

The exploits of the 8 Army and its men slid, as everything quickly does, from the front page to the history book; the young men grew old, and the tanks and trucks and guns were scrapped and melted down. Even though all the faces and all the weapons changed in the British Army, still it had learned something and added to the rich traditions of British men-at-arms. New enemies stepped on the stage, swaggered about, and departed.

After World War II, all British infantry regiments were reduced to a single battalion of regulars, an effort to maintain the long and satisfying tradition of regimental affiliation

Soldiers from 7 Platoon, G Company, 2 Battalion, The Scots Guards greet the news of the Argentine collapse on 14 June 1982. They aren't pretty, but then the *previous night they took the strongly defended Mount Tumbledown at the point of bayonet.* Paul Haley, Soldier Magazine, via Martin Windrow

that goes back nearly 300 years now. Of sixty-five regiments on the rolls at the end of World War II, only eleven were still around with their identities fully intact in 1989, and the prospects for survival after the demise of the Warsaw Pact threat was bleak.

A New Breed of Rat

For five decades 4 and 7 Armoured Brigades stared down a different adversary—the combined forces of the Warsaw Pact—in northern Europe. Luckily for all concerned nothing happened, but the years of training and preparation were not wasted after all. When Iraq invaded Kuwait in the summer of 1989, fifty years after the original Rat pack set to work, the Iraqis were promptly opposed by a new generation of British soldier. Although many things had changed about the British Army, the Rats who went to fight in the Gulf had much in common

Crewing a modern British tank is still a demanding occupation. Tanks are still noisy, cramped, and dangerous. Armor is thicker, guns shoot farther and *harder, but the mission is essentially the same as it was a half-century ago on the battlefields of North Africa and Europe.* via Will Fowler

with the men of their grandfather's generation: a sense of humor, a tolerance for adversity, a casual approach to attire in the field, a commitment to completing missions—and a taste for strong tea.

Now, as in 1939, the British Army is a small, under-funded community of professional soldiers with high standards of military performance, diverse accents, and a variety of colors. Unlike the Rats of World War II, today's units include a number of women. The tanks travel faster, shoot harder and more accurately; the rifles look radically different; the food is much improved, but the profanity is about the same.

A half-century ago "Desert Rat" meant, initially, someone who served in 7 Armoured Division; then the term was adopted by all the 8 Army and its numerous subordinate units. When British forces went to the Gulf they all, once again, adopted the term regardless of pedigree. And so this book is about all the British forces that went to the Gulf—and the ones that didn't, too, by indirect fire. The Gulf war brought together a force that became a cohesive, professional, energetic, imaginative fighting force called the 1 (British) Armoured Division.

The entire British Army today is, as it was fifty-plus years ago, a small, professional force. Including the Parachute Regiment and all the other units, it is still smaller than the US Marine Corps—147,000 men and women, and shrinking down toward 116,000 by 1995. But despite its compact dimensions, this Army is (like its ancestor) an experienced, energetic, imaginative force with a talent for making large numbers of adversaries mind their manners, one way or another. It has demonstrated that it is among the very first rank of military organizations worldwide, in Korea, across Asia, in the Falklands, and most recently in the Gulf. It accomplishes this stature by maintaining extremely high standards for admission and even higher standards for training of its units. British Paras, for example, endure a six-month program that is the approximate equal of American Ranger, Special Forces, and Airborne training all rolled into one. The actual numbers of

British infantry no longer wears the scarlet tunic into battle, but the challenges for today's "Private Thomas Atkins" are quite similar to those of two and three hundred years ago—suppressing insurrections, disorders, and enemies, foreign and domestic. via Will Fowler

British soldiers may be small but for many reasons, including tradition, training, and doctrine, the whole force is the legitimate heir to the Rats of a half-century ago.

The Regiment

The legendary British Army regiment is a cultural institution not duplicated, except in name, in American Army units. As British military historian and publisher Martin Windrow says, "The infantry regiment isn't merely a tactical unit. It is an identity, a depot, with an honorary colonel and a collective legend. This regiment can never be killed by the enemy even if all the field battalions are wiped out. The identity is simply adopted by the new recruits, sucking on the mythical tit of the remaining depot, a few home cadre, the legend."

These regiments are actually only single battalions, with perhaps 500 or 600 soldiers in peacetime, infantry regiments being expandable during war. Cavalry (armor) regiments are always single-battalion in size. Both infantry and cavalry regiments use the battalion for tactical and administrative functions. An American Marine Corps regiment, by contrast, is a huge assembly of three big battalions, with associated supporting units, that can easily reach strengths of 7,000 or more people—but without quite so much lore, legend, or the variety of names and uniforms.

Overview

In 1991, the entire British Army included 147,000 people serving around the world. Of these, 7,000 were Gurkhas, the famous tribal hill soldiers from Nepal who traditionally serve in Hong Kong and throughout Asia. The rest of the Army trains to fight anywhere around the world, with major troop commitments in many places to reinforce British foreign policy. While the bulk of this commitment has traditionally been in Germany, it was shifted to the Falklands in 1982 and to the Gulf in 1990.

BAOR

Most of the Army is, and has been committed to the British Army of the Rhine (BAOR) since the conclusion of World War II. There is an entire army corps there—a headquarters supporting the North Atlantic Treaty Organization (NATO) and a large cast of supporting players. The BAOR had, in 1991, twelve armored regiments, two recon regiments, and sixteen infantry battalions, supported by eight field artillery regiments, plus additional regiments with heavy artillery, missile, air defense, counterbattery location, and depth-fire missions, supported in turn by seven regiments of engineers and three army aviation units providing combat support and combat service support. The BAOR is a big commitment of people and equipment—and was just about milked dry to provide forces when Iraq invaded Kuwait.

Overseas Garrisons

Besides the postings to Germany, Britain has major commitments to Belize (a former colony coveted by its neighbor Guatemala), Brunei, Cyprus, the Falklands, Gibraltar, and Hong Kong. Smaller units serve in twenty-six nations as advisors, mostly in Africa and the Middle East.

As a result of England's colonial heritage, modern-day Desert Rats can find themselves

Service in Northern Ireland is part of the routine for British soldiers, a stressful and sometimes dangerous mission where the enemy doesn't wear a uniform or follow anybody's rules. British Army

posted to some extremely soggy locations where people sometimes shoot at visitors. Besides Belize, which hosts about 1,400 British soldiers (an infantry battalion, an armored recon company, a battery of artillery, and supporting units), another 1,500 British soldiers have the memorable experience of defending the Falklands from the "Argies," should they wish to try another invasion.

United Kingdom

Although most British combat armor and artillery units are deployed to Germany, most of the infantry battalions are kept at home. While part of the reason for this is economy, part is the need to rotate infantry units into Northern Ireland, a dangerous and stressful assignment that is part of the normal routine for latter-day Rats. There are thirty-one infantry battalions in the UK, plus a Gurhka battalion, seven artillery regiments, and eight combat support units, including the renowned Special Air Service (SAS) and the three battalions of the Parachute Regiment (Paras).

Northern Ireland

The long campaign against Irish Republican Army (IRA) terror in Ireland consumes a lot of attention for the British Army and provides a kind of real-world training that isn't available to other armies, which is just as well, because this conflict has been an exceptionally nasty one at times. Ten British infantry battalions serve in Northern Ireland: six resident battalions and four others that rotate through on short tours of about six months. Three brigades—3, 8, and 39—conduct operations in the six Ulster counties under the command of Headquarters, Northern Ireland, at Lisburn (near Belfast). Supporting the infantry is a squadron of SAS, plus two of engineers, an army air corps regiment, and nine battalions of the Royal Irish Regiment.

As unpleasant as service in Northern Ireland is, it provides a kind of low-level battle experience that American soldiers try to approximate at elaborate training grounds like the National Training Center (NTC) in California, where armor units rehearse their moves, and the Joint Readiness Training Center (JRTC) in Arkansas for infantry. Northern Ireland certainly lacks the intensity of these training facilities, with only occasional brief little encounters, but in Northern Ireland the opposing force uses real bullets and explosives and real people get killed. Fifteen British soldiers died during 1990 in Northern Ireland, 120 bombs were discovered, about two tons of explosives were detonated by the IRA, and 223 firearms were captured. Soldier skills are learned quickly and well in such a place.

A young infantryman/radio operator on patrol in Belfast, Northern Ireland. British Army

Chapter 1

History and Traditions

In a way, there is no one British Army with one history and tradition. The thing we call a British Army is in fact a lot of little bands of clan warriors, dressed up in modern kit, with SA80 rifles instead of swords and pikes. These clans no longer fight each other (except occasionally after a few beers, and then only because its traditional). But this is no homogenous collection of humanity as is the US Army pattern, and the institution is the richer for it.

The heritage of British Army units frequently is an ancient and revered one. The preservation of this tradition has evolved through complex ceremonials into something quite mythical. The formal drill that members of the Guards regiments perform are not for the amusement of tourists but a way of remembering its heritage and keeping its lessons alive. The story of the British Army today is found in the stories of its regiments that go back about 300 years.

For those who slept through their history lessons, the British Isles became home to many diverse little clans of peoples over the centuries,

The Queen's Birthday Parade in London on 11 June 1988. The Escort for the Colour is 1 Battalion Irish Guards. The red jacket was first issued as a universal uniform to the New Model Army in 1645. The Foot Guards' tall "bearskin" was awarded in 1815 to commemorate the Guards' defeat of Napoleon's bearskin-bonneted Imperial Guard at Waterloo. Martin Windrow

by gradual migration and invasion: Celts, Saxons, Britons, Danes, Scots, and all the rest, all on a rather small bit of real estate. These people clustered together in small kinship groups for defense (and occasional offense). When one group raided another—an extremely frequent occurrence—the local menfolk took up whatever weapons were available, selected a leader, and confronted the adversary. The pattern of recruitment by local lords persisted through medieval times during the many English civil wars, and local companies were gathered into national armies for the endless wars against the traditional enemy—France. In the eighteenth century, England's conventional standing army still fought all over the world in regiments raised under license, and partly paid for, by local aristocrats/colonels.

14/20 King's Hussars

For example, one of the units deployed to the Gulf, 14/20 King's Hussars, traces its pedigree back to July of 1715 when it was raised by James Dormer. The unit was called 14 or Dormer's Dragoons, and (like all dragoons) rode into battle and was equipped with musket, sword, and pistol. Dragoons fight from horseback as well as dismounted. Three months later the freshly trained farm boys fought a battle with the Jacobite rebels, finally suppressing the insurrection. In 1776 the unit became a part of the cavalry, an elite component of the Army then and now. Their mission became one of raiding

Captain Richard Bryson, Royal Artillery. The British Army "uniform" really isn't—there is considerable variation from one regiment to another, often from one individual to another. But the three black "pips" on the shoulder will always identify a captain, and the RA (Royal Artillery) and the artillery crest on the beret leave little doubt about where this cheerful young officer calls home.

and reconnaissance, and their arsenal acquired a kind of poled weapon called a hedging bill, along with the carbine, pistol, sabre, and bayonet.

As an example of the kind of thing that makes for a rich regimental history, 14's possibly most famous victory came while fighting the French at Vitoria, Spain, in 1813. There 14 captured Emperor Joseph Bonaparte's baggage train, and with it the silver chamber pot used by the enemy commander. That chamber pot is still owned by its captors who still use it—as a toasting cup.

The regimental history includes less amusing heritage, too. It was virtually wiped out shortly thereafter and has participated in many long, sad campaigns. In 1861 the regiment was converted to hussars, a kind of light cavalry, and went on to fight in Sudan and South Africa.

Number 14 was wedded to 20 Hussars, an amalgamation of two distinguished light cav-alry regiments during an earlier period of defense down-sizing. Number 20 Hussars were a good match for the 14; they had executed the last regimental cavalry charge in 1920, against Turkish nationalists, had fought long, hard, and well in the First World War, and had a long history of service in the Middle East.

It wasn't until 1938 that the King's Hussars were unhorsed, trading in their faithful animals for much less faithful but better armored vehicles just in time to be shipped off to Persia (now Iran). The mission, though, was much as it had always been: screening, raiding, reconnais-sance—just as it is today.

Since then, the combined regiment has served as part of the 8 Army in World War II, in Persia, Singapore, Hong Kong, Cyprus, Libya, and Germany. True to its tradition, the regiment has strong geographic roots; it recruits in Lancashire (in the English midlands), with most of its soldiers coming from the towns of Preston, Manchester, and Bolton.

The Staffordshire Regiment (The Prince of Wales')

Another distinguished element of the Rat pack are the Staffords, a fine old regiment that goes back to 1705 when Col. Luke Lillington started collecting local lads at the King's Head Hotel in Litchfield. He took the assembled multitude off to the West Indies, where the unit stayed for over fifty years battling the French and Spanish—and dying like flies from tropical diseases. Designated 38 Regiment of Foot from 1751, it went off to fight in the American War of Independence (never losing a battle), then in France, India, Holland, Egypt, and France again, against Napoleon. Then it was off to China, the Crimea, and many years of service in India. In 1879, it was shipped off to Africa to fight the Zulus.

When England joined the First World War, the redesignated South Staffordshire Regiment, and its sister North Staffords, ballooned tremendously, ultimately including thirty-five battalions. Ten thousand Staffords died in that war. Seven Staffords were awarded Britain's highest combat decoration, the Victoria Cross (VC).

During World War II, the regiment fought first in France, then in North Africa with the original Rats and on into Italy. Part of the regiment was sent to India and fought with the Chindit force into Burma while another part was converted to an air-landing battalion and fought at Arnhem where they became the only unit in the whole war to earn two VCs in one battle.

But after the war, along with other infantry regiments, the North and South Staffords were reduced to just a single battalion of regulars. Both were in military matrimony in 1959 while posted to Germany. The Staffords have continued their travels to Kenya, then to Uganda (suppressing a mutiny), back to the UK, and on to Honduras, Bahrain, and then to Northern Ireland.

Pomp and Circumstance

American units, to a limited degree, observe a few formal occasions; the US Marine Corps birthday on 11 November is the most notable of these, an occasion for formal dinners and dances, but the Corps is virtually unique in this respect. The Brits, on the other hand, cherish their high holy days and make the most of them. They are called "regimental days," and every regiment has one or more when ceremonies are observed and the unit may "troop the color."

The Staffords have two—and two alternates, in case of inclement weather! The days are Ypres Day (31 July) and Ferozeshah Day (21 December), and only one is normally celebrated—the first if in England, the latter if in the tropics somewhere. The first celebrates a successful attack during the First World War at the blood-letting of the same name in 1917, while the latter commemorates a bit of gallantry by 80 Foot (later incorporated into the Staffords) in 1845, during the first Sikh War.

The ceremony involves presentation of the regimental colors at a formal parade to a special Sergeant's Color Party. The colors are held by the noncommissioned officers until midnight, when they are returned with great ceremony to an officers color party at a formal dinner called the Sergeants' Ferozeshah Ball. All of this

honors the valor of Color Sergeant Matthew Kirkland who captured the battle flag of a Sikh unit during close combat. The sergeant was commissioned on the battlefield for his bravery—and the captured standard is still on display in the Stafford regimental chapel in Litchfield Cathedral.

Two other British regiments, the Duke of Wellington's Royal Regiment and the old East

Much of the training done by modern-day Desert Rats deals with the problems of urban combat. It is put to the test in Northern Ireland on combat patrols where British soldiers must deal with snipers, bombers, and rock-throwers.

Surrey Regiment have had similar ceremonies, likewise based on gallantry during the Sikh War of 1845.

Colors and Honors

Each British Army infantry regiment has two important flags for ceremonial occasions, a Regimental color and a Queen's color, one representing the unit and the other the monarch. Until the time of the First World War these flags were present on the battlefield and had an important communication function, a visible way for soldiers to locate their leaders in the confusion of combat. Capturing an enemy's colors was, as Sergeant Kirkland demonstrated, an act of tremendous military virtue. Loss of a regiment's colors to the enemy was a supreme disgrace.

Once the colors became obvious targets for accurate long-range artillery, the decision to be a bit more discreet was made, and these flags were displayed only during happier times. It's a tradition maintained by most armies, including American, Russian, and many others. On American battle flags, honors are recorded on ribbons attached to the top of the flag staff—battle streamers, they are called. British regimental colors have their honors embroidered directly on

A detail of a Guards uniform; the decoration identifies the soldier as Gulf War veteran. It is difficult to imagine wearing such a uniform in combat, but this pattern is a close replica of that worn by British soldiers of the past.

the flag. For regiments like the Staffords the flags can be quite crowded. The Stafford's regimental color bears forty battle honors for actions from 1759 to 1919 while their Queen's Color carries thirty-four honors from the two world wars. In fact, the regiment has more honors than flag; there are another sixty-six that are omitted for lack of space.

Titles, Badges, and Dress Distinctions

The history and heritage of individual regiments is a source of much pleasure and pride for many members of these old organizations. During the recent unpleasantness in the Gulf, individuals from many regiments were mixed and matched with those from others in task-organized specialist units. But even so, visitors were readily apparent to the observer because, while everybody might have the same basic uniform, berets and regimental insignia were retained from each individual's home regiment. Such identification is an important part of British Army corporate culture.

Some regiments, like the Staffords, have courtesy titles appended to their names, further confusing the American observer. Although known universally as the Staffords, the regiment's proper name is The Staffordshire Regiment (The Prince of Wales' Own). The latter part of this is an honor from Queen Victoria, bestowed in 1876 on an old regiment that was later amalgamated into the Staffords; their honor was incorporated, along with a bit of other symbolism, the plumes that are part of the Prince of Wales insignia, along with the tune, "God Bless the Prince of Wales," used by the regiment as its slow ceremonial march.

Further symbolism lies in the badge Staffords wear on berets, a Stafford knot with the previously mentioned plumes. The Staffords, of course, aren't the only ones with a distinctive beret, and in fact some latter-day Rats wear Highland caps with hackles or short feather plumes as part of their normal uniform.

Uniform and Kit

While we're discussing the British uniform it might be a good time to observe that, actually,

A mounted Guards Regiment soldier endures an hour on post near Whitehall in London. The principal danger of such duty comes from thoughtless tourists who poke and prod at the horses, pet them, and insist on having their pictures made while holding the bridle. According to one report, possibly apocryphal, one such tormenting tourist got a whack on the backside with the flat of a guard's sword for extremely thoughtless behavior.

there isn't one. The camouflaged battle dress and the khaki dress uniform are issued to all soldiers, but from there on, considerable variation is not just tolerated but prized. The headdress is the most noticeable tribal item; there are about eleven different shades of beret, all with distinctive badges, many with special color patches behind, and even feather hackles. The Scottish regiments retain the tam-o'-shanter, the Irish the green caubeen. Even on the working dress, regiments display special colored lanyards, badges of rank, and stable belts. On

Sergeant Brooks is a tanker from the Queen's Royal Irish Hussars and saw considerable combat in the Gulf.

dress uniforms units jealously preserve the badges and flashes commemorating ancient battles and old amalgamated regiments. In the cavalry this reaches a peak of sartorial glory with bright-colored trousers, chain-mail epaulettes, and some dazzling head gear. All this ancestor-worship naturally reinforces esprit de corps.

Battle dress in a combat area is notorious for its imaginative variety. Montgomery's 8 Army was a many-splendored thing, encouraged in part by the commander himself whose attire, from two-badge beret to sloppy corduroys, seldom included a single regulation item. British soldiers tend to augment regulation issue combat clothing with personally purchased "kit"— the generic Brit term for personal equipment of any kind. In the Gulf, all kinds of commercially acquired or traded foreign smocks, boots, load-bearing vests, and web gear were common. The Arab headscarfs or *shemagh* were actually issued by the Army, but by that time, most Brits had acquired their own in a range of colors.

Since desert warfare had not been an anticipated mission for the Brits prior to the Gulf war, the first troops to arrive, and the second line throughout the war, wore battle dress designed for jungle use, in green, brown, yellow, and black camouflage. Sand and brown desert combats and nuclear, biological, and chemical (NBC) suits were designed, made, and shipped to the fighting units before the ground war began.

Force Structure

The British Army, like any other, is a team built of tooth and tail organizations that provide mutual support. Although the "tooth" parts of the organism (the combat arms—armor, artillery, infantry, and so on) tend to get the glory (and pay for it with the bulk of the physical risk and discomfort), the "tail" (logistics and medical support, communications, etc.) keeps the whole thing alive.

Cavalry

Although cavalry is as old as warfare, the modern variety is armored. The British version is profoundly traditional. There are twenty regiments of cavalry, all but four with lineage that go far back into history and to the days of horses. The names of these regiments include echoes of that era when dragoons, hussars, and lancers were the modern mobile combat arm for screening, recon, raids, and skirmishing. The horses were put out to pasture in the 1930s in exchange for tanks, scout cars, and light armored vehicles, but the names were retained.

The cavalry accounts for about eight percent of the manpower of the British Army but far more than that in terms of combat power. It is the dominant element of the army, like its American and Russian equivalents, and consumes a large slice of available funding.

Infantry

Almost one-third of the British Army is composed of infantry regiments. Like other modern armies it has two major variations: light and mechanized. Every time the armchair strategists decide that infantry is redundant and no longer needed on the battlefield, along comes a war to prove otherwise. The Israelis discovered this the hard way in the Yom Kippur war when their tanks, operating without infantry support, were eaten alive by the Arab armies' infantry using Soviet-supplied Sagger anti-tank missiles. And British Paras demonstrated the utility of light infantry with the Royal Marines and

A section of infantry assaults in the elaborate "Impossible City" used for FIBUA training at the Combined Arms Training Centre near Warminster, in the west- *England county of Wiltshire. The training is extremely intense, challenging and dangerous.*

3 Para's epic, brilliant yomp (as they call a forced march) across sixty miles of boggy, frigid countryside, under 100-pound packs at the battle for Goose Green during the Falklands campaign, achieving the impossible and breaking the enemy's will to resist.

Currently, the fifty-five battalions of regular infantry are slated to be reduced to thirty-eight by 1997. These are augmented by Territorial Army battalions and reserves, also scheduled for reduction.

Artillery

Traditionally, artillery is the major killer on the battlefield. It combines art and science. About 10 percent of the British Army is contained in the artillery regiments. Although they don't get the glory of the more prestigious

Ready for patrol in the Belfast, Northern Ireland, combat zone. One of the reasons that British Army soldiers train hard and long is because they have been going off to fight in a nasty little urban war within the British Isles. Kevin Lyles

organizations, within the Army the artillery is considered to be extremely professional and is well-respected. The foundation for this service in the British Army is the Royal Regiment of Artillery (RA), a corps with twenty-nine numbered artillery regiments on line.

Combat Engineers

Another support arm, the engineers have an extremely important and dangerous mission that seldom gets the glory of the tankers or

The combat kit of today is considerably less gaudy. The sabre has been exchanged for the Light Support Weapon (LSW), a light machine gun. Today's British soldier makes for a more difficult target than his conspicuous ancestor.

A Guardsman walks his post near Parliament. The tremendous pride that many British citizens feel about their history and heritage is maintained by these displays.

infantry. About 9 percent of the British Army is in the engineer regiments. These units are essential in attack and defense, their missions being to enhance the mobility of the friendly units and to restrict the movement of the enemy. The engineers move forward with the mobile bridges to get the tanks across ditches and creeks, clear the minefields, and dig the fighting positions for armor and infantry.

Signals
The signals units provide communication between units and commanders, a vital element of modern command and control. Much of the expense of modern military forces goes into the development and acquisition of radios, microwave communication systems, radars, and advanced technologies like fiber-optic cables that help commanders command.

Army Aviation
British Army aviation support is provided by both the Royal Air Force and by the Army itself, with the RAF supplying the heavy lift and the Army aviation regiments assigned to recon, liaison, medium troop lift, and anti-armor at-

The Chieftain main battle tank on exercises in Germany. The Chieftain is now a second-line system used primarily for training armor crewmen, with the Challenger being Britain's first-line main battle tank (MBT). The Chieftain has been in service since 1967 although it is a 1950s set of technologies. Like the American M60, it has been upgraded over the years and is still a formidable weapon although it (like the M60) is generally regarded as obsolete. The gun is extremely accurate even at ranges out to six miles, far beyond normal engagement ranges. Will Fowler

tack missions. Six regiments will be available under restructuring, one of which will be assigned to Northern Ireland.

Transport

The Royal Corps of Transport are the truck drivers of the army, delivering everything to everybody everywhere. Fifteen regiments are currently dedicated to the logistics support mission, four of which will be eliminated during the next few years.

Ordnance

The Royal Ordnance Supply Corps supplies the hardware and consumables that keep an army in the field: fuel, ammunition, and spare parts that the Royal Corps of Transport delivers. The ROSC is structured as twelve battalions currently, but will shrink to ten or so.

Medical

Every major command includes a staff to provide immediate medical care for combat

FIBUA training. These soldiers are aiming a sniper position with a Carl Gustav 84mm rocket launcher. The Carl Gustav was originally designed for killing main battle tanks and still would defeat the armor of tanks like the many old tanks fielded by the Iraqis but would hardly scratch the paint on most modern MBTs. The Carl Gustav fires a wide variety of ammu-nition and is accurate and effective out to 400 meters for a moving target like a truck, but has a tremendous backblast that makes it a very obvious target after the first round is fired. It is still useful as a bunker-buster and against trucks and light armor, but it is being replaced by the Light Antitank Weapon (LAW). Will Fowler

41

casualties, which is part of a much larger medical establishment that includes over 500 doctors and several thousand medical support staff to handle the sick and wounded.

Reserves

The British Army has two reserve systems, the Territorial Army (TA) and the Reserve. About 186,000 men and women currently serve in the Regular Army Reserves. The Reserve includes several classifications with different functions. Officers separated from active service remain members of the Regular Reserve and are liable for call-up until the age of fifty-five. The Long-Term Reserve and Army Pensioners are also liable for call-up. Most of these aren't members of regular training units but would serve as battle casualty replacements in the event of a general war.

The TA is an evolution of the old Volunteer Battalions, formed in 1908. The TA has a close relationship with many of the Regular regiments, to which units are affiliated, and a rich history of combat experience in both world wars. There are currently about 72,000 people in the TA, but that number will become smaller as

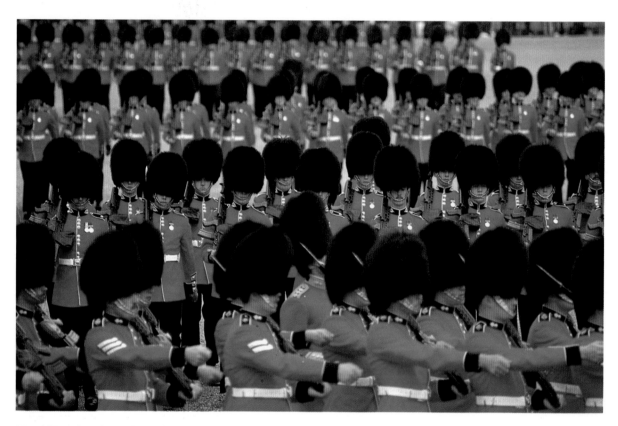

The 2 Battalion Scots Guards march past on one of the high holy days of the British Army, the Queen's Birthday. Foot Guards battalions perform public ceremonial duties in London on rotation tours; the rest of their service is spent as normal combat infantry. Several of these men display medals for active duty in Northern Ireland and the Falklands. With very few exceptions British soldiers and officers of junior rank are awarded medals only for active service—they don't have many decorations but the ones they wear are earned. Martin Windrow

units are disbanded or amalgamated. The reduction is unfortunate because the reserves normally include some of the most experienced and able soldiers in any army.

The TA mission is complex: during a large war, the TA would provide all home-defense forces, plus a significant portion of the BAOR manpower. It is heavy in infantry and provides two of the three SAS regiments, plus three parachute battalions. The TA also includes signals, artillery, transport, and cavalry regiments, usually linked to regular regiments.

The TA soldiers all serve a two-week summer camp period plus another thirty days during the course of the year, for which they receive the same daily pay as Regulars, plus an annual bonus that increases in value with length of service.

Officers

What does it take to be an officer in the British Army? Well, according to the troops who follow

Warrant Officer 2 "Rooster" Barber, wears the maroon beret of the Parachute Regiment—and the sweet-natured, generous expression that goes with his sergeant-major's job. Actually, the sergeant-major (like others of the breed) is extremely charming, friendly, and attends to the needs of the enlisted soldiers in his care. People who achieve this exhalted rank, in any army, tend to be highly intelligent and efficient leaders and managers with a talent for getting people to do things.

A young platoon leader, Second Lieutenant N. P. Rhodes, is one of those rare British officers who come up from the ranks. He is a member of the Duke of Wellington's Regiment (West Riding).

43

them, a British Army officer has to have 1) a Volvo, 2) a signet ring, 3) an odd accent, and 4) a yellow dog, preferably a golden retriever. There is considerable accuracy in this observation, but

This fledgling second lieutenant's rank is visible only on the small tab on the front of his combat smock, the single star or "pip" worn by new officers. He commands a platoon of infantry and is here briefing them for a house-clearing exercise.

it leaves out a lot. For one thing, serving the British nation as an Army officer is still a prestigious career with status in the United Kingdom, and one that attracts people of considerable stature (who, in the United States might go into law or medicine but never the profession of arms). While not all officers are from the British upper classes, as the list of requirements mentioned previously suggests, many are. They earn a great deal of loyalty and respect for their choice. The Queen's son, Prince Andrew, served in the Navy. Most male members of the Royal family are still expected to graduate in at least one of the armed services and to serve with units for at least a few years. Prince Charles is a qualified paratroop officer, RAF pilot, and once commanded a Royal Navy warship. Prince Andrew flew Navy helicopters in combat in the Falklands. This tradition of service by all social classes makes the British Army more democratic and inclusive in ways than the US Army.

As with American forces, there are many ways to acquire a commission. There is a university cadet program similar to the Reserve Officer Training Course (ROTC) program in the United States, another program for enlisted soldiers who wish to become commissioned, and yet another program for young men and women who decide early to make the Army a career.

In the case of the latter program, a typical individual would finish high school with two A-level exams—high scores on advanced academic tests that are somewhat similar to American Scholastic Aptitude Test scores. Instead of enrolling in a university, a young man (for example), typically about nineteen, would apply for a commission in a particular local regiment or corps. If found qualified by initial screening, he would go before the Regular Commissions Board at Westbury, in Wiltshire. If selected by the Board, he would then be sent to Sandhurst, the Royal Military Academy (RMA), for a six-month course of instruction.

Sandhurst, by contrast with West Point, doesn't pretend to offer a general education in engineering and the humanities; there is no football team and few recreational activities. Sandhurst teaches the military fundamentals of leadership in battle and the best ways to kill people and destroy things. Until recently there were two courses at the RMA, a six-month short course for short-term officers, and a longer, one-year program for career officers; as a result of the recent down-sizing, the course is now only offered as a six-month program. On completion, the graduate is commissioned a second lieutenant in the Army and will begin what is normally a twenty-two-year career.

As is the case in the United States, the young officer will go through a cycle of postings that provide a wide range of experience and training—and that offer the Army the chance to evaluate and perhaps fire the officer if he or she is not up to standard. Typically, this will include command experience at the platoon and company level, advanced military schools, staff postings, deployments overseas and to Northern Ireland, and perhaps as an exchange officer to a foreign army.

Typically, the young subaltern (as the second lieutenant is called) will command a platoon. During this command, the officer begins to really learn the craft, largely from the senior sergeants and older officers in the company. An officer is watched closely; leadership of soldiers is more art than science and not something that can be learned in school. Otherwise talented subalterns, perhaps with marvelous technical skills, often turn out to be quite unsuitable for command—and they are let go, gently sometimes, sometimes not.

If successful, the young officer will be promoted to lieutenant, then to captain and posted as second-in-command to a company or troop. At this point the officer goes back to school for courses at the Junior Division of the Staff College at Warminster as preparation for work in battalion and brigade staffs. The young captain then takes the test for promotion to major and is again evaluated. If considered suitable, the major is off to school again, to the Command and Staff Course at the Staff College at Camberley for a year of study.

Surviving the Command and Staff Course makes the officer eligible for further promotion into the senior ranks of the Army. Once an officer becomes a major, further promotion is done through peer-review committees, selection boards made up of other officers. Lieutenant colonels are sent to the National Defence College at Latimer for a six-month program, and those few, favored individuals who are selected to become brigadiers attend the Royal College of Defence Studies.

Approximately 1,300 individuals sign on for officer training each year, while about 1,800 officers return to "civvy street." Officer pay ranges from £11,763 for new second lieutenants, rising to about £23,000 for a captain and about £37,000 for a senior lieutenant colonel. A brigadier receives £50,000. The officer corps of the British Army is shrinking along with the rest of the establishment, declining from a current number of about 16,000 officers to an estimated 11,000 by 1995.

Rank and File

The enlisted soldiers may once have been the scum of the earth, as Wellington observed, but selection and retention standards are considerably higher today. The enlisted ranks of the British Army, as in the US Army, frequently include a few college graduates and the occasional Ph.D. But most of the lads have come from a working-class background. In the United Kingdom, school students have the choice of leaving school at age sixteen or seventeen and entering trade programs or the military or continuing, if their O-level test scores are high enough, on to university.

Unemployment has been worse in the United Kingdom since World War II than in the United States, so service in the armed forces has been an attractive option for many young men and women. As a result, the Army has the ability to pick and choose the best candidates and to eject people who don't measure up during training. In the British Army, choosing and ejecting happens more than in the US Army.

About 35 percent of new recruits come out of school as juniors after a careful screening process. The new enlistee is tested and assigned to a training program and a regiment. Training is done at special technical schools and at the training depots operated by the administrative divisions, and normally lasts about four and one-half months. Only about 70 percent of the recruits survive the entire course; some quit and others are rejected as unsuitable.

Life in the regiments, as in modern military units everywhere, involves an intense routine of training: physical fitness, tactical, and techni-cal. One of the virtues of the regimental system is that a soldier can't easily escape a bad reputa-tion by a posting to a different unit, as is the case in other armies. For better or worse, a soldier's career is tied up for twenty-two years with his or her mates in the regiment.

Promotion is based on tests and course work. Rank comes slowly; a soldier can expect to

Second Lieutenant N. P. Rhodes and a few of his band of merry men: Lance Corporal Carter, Lance Corporal O'Neill, Private Stansfield and Private Martin.

remain a private until promotion to lance corporal after about four years service. The rank of corporal and command of a section is the next step and usually comes after about six years. Sergeants will have about ten years in the Army at the time of promotion and will then become the noncommissioned officer running a platoon —teaching the trade to new subalterns, who nominally command the platoon. Staff sergeants will be promoted after about thirteen years; good ones go on to become warrant officers in a couple of years, and perhaps eventually to the typically revered grade of regimental sergeants major. The RSM is a warrant officer but remains (unlike his US Army counterpart) a noncommissioned officer rather than a member of the officer's mess.

Soldiers receive anywhere from £7,300 per year at the lowest recruit level to £13,000 for a lance corporal in pay band 2 (the British system is based on rank plus skill group). Sergeants are paid about £16,000. The RSM, who's earned it, gets about £20,000. These basic rates of pay are augmented with housing allowances for married soldiers, payment for meals, and long-service bonuses.

Instead of the old system of a fixed duration of service contracts, the British soldier now signs up for what is called an open-engagement contract of twenty-two years from the age of eighteen or enlistment, whichever is later. After three years service and twelve months' notice— and barring a war in progress—a soldier can quit the Army for a shot at civilian life. It is fairly easy to return, and many young soldiers do just that.

The ranks will be thinning again, with a decline among the numbers of regular enlisted soldiers from a current 124,000 to around 96,000 by the middle of the 1990s. How this small force will be able to cope with the routine of army training, the responsibilities in Germany, Northern Ireland, Belize, Cyprus, all the other overseas postings, plus the occasional United Nations peace-keeping duties, remains to be seen. What also remains to be seen is how well the small armies of the future will cope with the real-world emergencies like the Falklands and the invasion of Kuwait.

It is a good system that produces, still, a soldier respected by every army around the world as skilled in all the elements of the trade. And while the officers may have pinkie rings and Volvos, you can usually spot the career British soldier in the crowd—he's the one with the odd accent and a couple of front teeth missing.

Chapter 2

The Thin Red Line: Infantry and Mechanized Infantry

They came here in the morning, looked over the wall, walked over it, killed all the garrison, and retired for breakfast.—Observations of an enemy commander in India after an encounter with the British infantry in 1803.

The British infantry is the best in the world; fortunately, it is not numerous.—French commander General Bugeaud, watching the English prepare to attack his forces during the Peninsular campaign, 1812.

They are really the scum of the earth and it is really wonderful that we should have made of them the fine fellows they are. With such an army we can go anywhere and do anything.—Wellington commenting on his own army's performance in the war with France, 1808–1814.

Of the English I would say, they stand by one another, and are often seen to die together. They are spirited enough, and have plenty of boldness. They are brave in fighting and full of resolution. They are the best of archers. Abroad, if things are going in favor of the enemy, they preserve good military discipline; and at all times are jovial yet quick in pride.—Robert Fluid, 1617.

. . . that day the Guards Brigade had evacuated Knightsbridge, after the area had been subjected all the morning to the combined fire of

A private from the Duke of Wellington's Regiment prepares to assault an "enemy" position in a building during intense training at the Combined Arms Training Centre.

every piece of artillery we could bring to bear. This brigade was practically a living embodiment of the positive and negative qualities of the British soldier—an extraordinary bravery and toughness was combined with a rigid inability to move quickly.—Rommel, 13 June 1943 (just before El Alamein).

I have seen what I never thought to be possible—a single line of infantry break through three ranks of cavalry ranked in order of battle, and tumble them to ruin.—Marquis de Contades, French commander at the battle of Minden, 1 August 1759.

If ever a people or a nation exemplified the phrase "brave to a fault" it is the British. If they had been less brave, there would have been many fewer faults and more victories. Caution they have not; they just bunt ahead and take the consequences.—Captain Solcum, US Army observer in a report on the Boer War, 1902.

How beautifully those English fight! But they MUST give way!—Napoleon at Waterloo, 1815.

Modern infantry is an amazing weapon. In fact, many in the profession of arms consider infantry—the common foot soldier, usually armed with a rifle—the ultimate weapon, the only thing that ultimately wins wars. Air power did far more to deliver on its old promise of strategic importance in the Gulf war than ever before, but when it came time to resolve the issue and complete the mission, mechanized infantry teamed with armor did the job.

That infantry should still exist at all is the historian's surprise. It is essentially a primitive, blunt instrument hardly changed, at the human level, during the last four thousand years. We use rifles now that reach farther and hit harder than the rocks, clubs, spears, or arrows of the distant past, but the tactical idea behind their use is identical. The formations and tactics of infantry units, as well as their sizes, is much the same now as in Caesar's legions. Infantry soldiers carry about the same load, about as far, on the march. They still come from about the same part of society, as do their leaders. It is a primitive, primal business.

On the hillsides around the British Army's Combined Arms Training Centre out in the west of England in Wiltshire are the remnants of fortifications built more than two thousand years ago. Those positions closely resemble those built by Iraqis, Americans, and Brits during the Gulf war. Although these defensive positions don't offer protection from indirect-fire weapons, many would be useful today. Infantry is like that, timeless in many ways.

And despite all the modern electronic warfare systems, missiles, tank technology, and "smart" bombs, the ultimate weapon for the British or any other nation is its common foot soldier, the infantryman. That's a fact that has to be re-learned every few decades. History has proven it to be true after the First World War, again after the Second, and several times since.

The British Army, like that of all other modern nations, is based on a combined-arms doc-

A British infantryman bringing in Argentine prisoners in the Falklands. Note his bulky night-vision sight—outclassed by the US-made equipment enjoyed by the enemy in a campaign during which nearly all combat took place during the night. Paul Haley/ Soldier Magazine

trine that integrates many different kinds of tooth and tail units into a cohesive force. After World War II and the development of nuclear weapons and intercontinental bombers and missiles, many political and military observers concluded that the need for armies in general and infantry in particular were part of the past. The postwar restructuring put most financial assets in big-buck technologies for aircraft and naval forces, pretty much to the neglect of the ground forces. But then current events, in Borneo, Korea, Malaya, Aden, Uganda, and far too many other places, showed that infantry wasn't quite obsolete, after all.

And it was well that they were retained because, when Argentina invaded the Falklands in 1982, across ten thousand miles of Atlantic, there was no better way of reasoning with the Argies than through the well-developed interpersonal communication skills of the British infantry, particularly the Royal Marines and the Paras. Once the Brits actually had a chance to

A group from 2 Para photographed after the enemy surrender at Goose Green, the Falklands. Crown Copyright

meet the Argies face to face and explain matters (mostly with their rifles, bayonets, machine guns, and mortars), it was only a short time until the Argentine Army decided it didn't really want those soggy islands after all.

Infantry can do that—when it is good—better, safer, cheaper, and with less bloodshed than any other military operation. But, as the Argentines learned most bitterly, good infantry is both born and made. It is a combination of mostly intangible, very human characteristics that can't be bought, manufactured, or induced through training. It takes a combination of

physical and emotional strengths, plus some wisdom, teamwork, and good doctrine to make a good field infantryman. Finding and developing those characteristics are the hard part—the modern weapons and the handsome uniforms are the easy part. And, through tradition, culture, and many other forces, nobody makes better infantrymen than the Brits.

The Wiring Diagram

The British Army is comprised of fifty-five battalions of infantry, although this may be reduced to about twenty by 1995. These are

Tough British training makes for tough British soldiers when the bullets start to fly. The ability of British soldiers and Royal Marines to carry 100-pound Bergen's on long "yomps" across the soggy Falklands terrain were not understood by the Argentine commanders. As a result the Argentines were thoroughly outclassed and overwhelmed despite many tactical advantages. via Martin Windrow

gathered into clans of regiments of one to three battalions, and the regiments are then assembled into eight administrative divisions. Two separate operational divisions, 1 Armoured and 3 Division, are combat formations. These divisions provide training for new recruits and manage all the personnel functions required to administer large groups of people conducting military operations.

Guards Division—eight battalions of Regulars
Scottish Division—seven battalions of Regulars
Queen's Division—nine battalions of Regulars
King's Division—eight battalions of Regulars
Prince of Wales' Division—nine battalions of Regulars
Light Division—six battalions of Regulars

Each of the administrative divisions has its own character and identity. The Guards, for example, have their own standards for new recruits. The Guards regiments are used for ceremonial duties as well as combat operations. As a result you will never see a "weedy" little Guardsman or one with glasses; only very tall, muscular blokes need apply. In fact, the Guards discriminate, as do many other British regiments, on the basis of size, color, and national origin, in addition to the usual standards. The British Army makes no apologies for formalizing ancient associations, and it certainly makes for an army with a lot of stylish variation.

The Foot Guards, along with the Horse Guards, are the elite of the army, emulated in

British infantry learn the fine art of urban combat at the "Impossible City." The grenades provide a satisfying "bang" without shredding the players.

many ways. Their drill is superb. They're snobby as hell. The rest of the army regards them with mixed feelings.

The Scottish Division has its own exclusivity. While Americans tend to think of the British Isles as a kind of homogenous mass of humanity, all who live there know otherwise. Scotland was a separate nation until the eighteenth century—and still is, in many ways. The clans of the north furnish some of the finest infantry in the army, with musical names and fearsome reputations: The Royal Scots (The Royal Regiment), The Royal Highland Fusiliers (Princess Margaret's Own Glasgow and Ayrshire Regiment), The King's Own Scottish Borderers, The Black Watch (Royal Highland Regiment), and many others. The Scots have traditionally performed with superb skill and courage, particularly during the two world wars, and again in the Gulf.

The British Army usually links an active duty battalion (the Regulars) with one or more battalions of reservists (members of the Territorial Army, called TAs). During wartime the TAs are activated and augment the Regular battalions. For example, within the Queen's Division is the Queen's Regiment; 1, 2, and 3 Battalions are Regulars while two others, 5 and 6/7 are TA. Here's the anatomy of the Queen's Division:

This sniper has spent considerable effort embellishing his "kit" and is an expert at blending into the landscape.

54

1, 2, & 3 Battalions—The Queen's Regiment
1, 2, & 3 Battalions—The Royal Regiment of
Fusiliers
1, 2, & 3 Battalions—The Royal Anglian
Regiment

Independent Infantry Regiments

Besides the regular divisions of infantry, there are several infantry regiments that operate independently.

Parachute Regiment

The legendary Paras are one of these, with three Regular battalions and three of TAs. The Paras are only about fifty years old, developed during World War II. The exploits of the regiment, at Tunisia, Normandy, Arnhem, the Rhine crossing, and everywhere else they fought, are legendary.

The mission of the Paras is that of light infantry—foot-mobile, self-sufficient, with

A member of the Irish Rangers during live fire exercises in Canada prepares to play his role in the grand production. Like snipers everywhere, he wears *a ghillie suit that he will have made himself.* via Martin Windrow

'plain' - n. large area of level country: devoid of hills.

Kevin Lyles' charming cartoons are often found in the British Army's official magazine, Soldier. *Kevin's little hero is the traditional British soldier, known for at least two hundred years by the name Tommy Atkins. Tom, in this particular exercise, is out training on the Salisbury Plain in the west of England; as the heavily burdened infantry soldier knows best, it is a very hilly sort of plain.* Kevin Lyles

man-portable weapons and a dearth of support from anybody else. This is not a place for the weak in body or spirit. Acceptance standards are extremely high. The course of instruction is long, demanding, and brutal. Attrition is also high, with about half surviving the six-month program. Parachuting is only a small part of the business that is intended to develop superb infantry who go to work by air; the parachute is merely a delivery device. Jumps are initially—and horrifyingly—made from a tethered balloon, later from aircraft.

This program is far more demanding than the one that produces American paratroopers, a three-week short course that graduates almost all its students—including a lot of old men and some chubby men and women. The standards of the US Army Basic Airborne School were lowered in the 1970s in order to include women in the program and as a result the prestige of an American maroon beret (identical to the British version on which it is based) was diminished. The British Army has made no such adjustments.

Brigade of Gurkhas

The brigade of Gurkhas is another equally exclusive and legendary band; while you may have to be tall (and Caucasian, too) to join the Guards, you'll have to be short and dark to join the Gurkhas. These little hill tribesmen come from Nepal, where service in the Gurkha regiments—a unique mercenary troop surviving from the old colonial days—is considered a high honor and where competition for admission to units with names like 2 Battalion, King Edward VII's Own Gurkha Rifles (The Sirmoor Rifles) is intense. These soldiers have traditionally been among the most dangerous for Britain's enemies. Sadly, by 1997 there are likely to be only two Gurkha battalions left, much to the disappointment of many in Nepal—and in England where these people are generally adored by their officers and by British civilians alike.

SAS Regiment

"We'd like to tell you about the Special Air Service . . . but if we did, we'd have to kill you." That's the joke about the SAS (and every other special operations force, for that matter, in any army—Spetsnaz, the Russian equivalent, probably says the same thing). The SAS is, like the American Delta and Spetsnaz, a kind of super infantry used only for the most demanding missions. These missions typically include counterterrorist operations, hostage rescue, raids, deep recon, and what is euphemistically called "target interdiction" missions. The last is a polite way of describing the work of the long-range sniper who, with an accurate rifle, powerful sight, and extensive training, can kill an enemy with the first shot at ranges exceeding a kilometer.

The SAS, like the US Army's Green Berets, is a direct descendant from a World War II program, in this case from David Stirling's desert raiders during the North African campaign. Using light vehicles, the Sterling force raided deep behind the lines on missions that could last many weeks. The resulting chaos forced the Afrikakorps to divert considerable resources to attempt to counter these raiders. The SAS participated in the Falklands campaign, as well as many other less-publicized actions. In the Falklands at least two squadrons of SAS troopers were deployed, one for recon missions, the other for raids. SAS units were ashore on the Falklands for weeks before the actual invasion, providing reconnaissance.

Despite all the pictures you see of these guys, they don't actually go around with black tape over their eyes, it's just a way to make visual identification of SAS members more difficult. Security is a serious subject in the SAS, unlike in some American special operations units that go around with decals, ball caps, and T-shirts proclaiming the affiliation of the owner.

We can tell you this much: SAS troopers are mostly accomplished linguists, superb combat marksmen, experienced parachutists specializing in the more exotic insertion techniques, and trained in a wide variety of explosives, unarmed-combat techniques, urban-combat skills, deep-recon procedures, space age communications, and all the other military ways to win friends and influence people.

The SAS includes three regiments: one Regular (22) and two TA (21 and 23). The regiments each include at least 400 troopers in four or five squadrons of about one hundred men each. The squadrons are built around troops of sixteen men each; within each troop are four-man teams. Each of the teams normally specializes in a particular skill: mountain, amphibious or urban operations, parachute insertion, recon, or demolitions.

The Regular regiment, 22 Regiment is unique in the SAS for its counterterrorist missions. In a rare public display of its bag of tricks, elements

The "Impossible City" is designed to challenge infantry squads and platoons with plenty of the kind of problem they will encounter in real urban combat, including inconvenient entrances for buildings that have to be cleared.

Squads must enter this building through a second-story window that is about five feet beyond the top of the ladder. They must make the entry while wearing full kit and with their weapons. The result is a very dangerous but realistic challenge where a slip can easily result in a serious injury.

of 22 Regiment relieved the siege on the Iranian embassy in London in 1980, broadcast live on television. During the course of eleven minutes, the embassy was "taken down," the six militants were killed, and their nineteen captives were released.

Infantry Regiments

Guards Division
The Grenadier Guards
The Coldstream Guards
The Scots Guards
The Irish Guards
The Welsh Guards

The Scottish Division
The Royal Scots
The Royal Highland Fusiliers
The King's Own Scottish Borderers
The Black Watch
The Queen's Own Highlanders
The Gordon Highlanders
The Argyle & Sutherland Highlanders

The King's Division
The King's Own Royal Border Regiment
The King's Regiment
The Prince Of Wales' Own Regiment Of Yorkshire
The Green Howards
The Royal Irish Regiment
The Queen's Lancashire Regiment
The Duke Of Wellington's Regiment
The Devonshire & Dorset Regiment
The Cheshire Regiment
The Royal Welsh Fusiliers
The Royal Regiment Of Wales
The Glouchestershire Regiment
The Worcestershire & Sherwood Foresters Regiment
The Royal Hampshire Regiment
The Staffordshire Regiment
The Duke Of Edinburgh's Royal Regiment

The Light Division
The Light Infantry
The Royal Green Jackets

The Brigade of Gurkhas
King Edward VII's Own Gurkha Rifles

The Queen Elizabeth's Own Gurkha Rifles
The 7th Duke Of Edinburgh's Own Gurkha Rifles
The 10th Princess Mary's Own Gurkha Rifles

Infantry Basics

As in other armies, the British infantry is of two basic types, light and mechanized. The first is more traditional and is expected to walk to work, carrying its tools of the trade; the Paras are one example of modern light infantry. The second and more common mechanized infantry rides to work in armored personnel carriers and is equipped and trained to work closely with armor.

Each has its own virtues and vices. Light infantry can be delivered very quickly to a battlefield. Since it doesn't own a lot of heavy equipment or very much artillery, it is comparatively easy to get it to the scene of the crime in a hurry. The down side is its vulnerability when it arrives, particularly if the enemy has a competent squadron or two of tanks. So light infantry is good for situations that rely on speed and surprise, and where the force can be either quickly withdrawn or reinforced. Typically, this means the seizure of airfields for follow-on forces. But should the initial mission fail, the force will be in trouble.

Mechanized infantry, though, is only about as agile as a few hundred armored vehicles can ever be. It takes much longer to put the force on the ground, and it takes a lot of logistic support to keep it fat and happy. But, with tanks and air support that know their business, a good mechanized infantry and armor team will rule the ground it stands on. British Challenger tanks are a match for any armor in the world, with a gun that has scored first-shot kills at three miles and frontal armor that will probably shed any projectile, but are themselves vulnerable to the enemy infantry who can pop up out of their holes with anti-tank guided missiles (ATGM) for shots from the flank or rear.

The job of the mechanized infantry is to ride along behind the tanks on an assault and then to "debuss" the personnel carriers and clear enemy positions when they are encountered. Only in-

The first "squaddie" up the ladder tosses a couple of grenades in the room, hauls himself up and inside, then hoses the interior with his rifle. Then the next man is helped up. When all are inside, the building is cleared from the top down to the cellar.

fantry is really effective at this job and it must be done the old-fashioned way, with rifle, bayonet, and grenade.

Infantry Organization and Employment

Battalion

The mechanized infantry battalions of the British Army are organized quite similarly to those fielded by other NATO nations, and former Warsaw Pact armies, too, for that matter. The battalion is the smallest combat command likely to conduct independent operations on a conventional battlefield. The British mechanized infantry version includes about 800 people and ninety-five lightly armored vehicles. The battalion commander is normally a lieutenant colonel supported by a staff and administrative team, the Headquarters Company that manages pay, promotions, communications ("signals" the Brits call it), medics, and other functions.

The essence of the battalion is its rifle companies. Since the battalion is based on what is called the triangular pattern, there are three of these companies, each with three platoons, and three sections in each platoon.

A non-commissioned officer instructs a platoon of reservists about to run the obstacle course at the Combined Arms Training Centre.

The battalion is vulnerable to a heavily armored enemy, a situation mitigated by a fourth company dedicated to fire support. The fire-support company normally has three platoons, as do the rifle companies, but these include an 81mm mortar platoon, a recon ("recce" the Brits call it) platoon mounted in Scimitar armored personnel carriers (APCs), plus another platoon with the battalion's anti-armor missiles, the twenty-four MILAN antitank-missile teams.

Battalion Mission

Infantry battalions are seldom suitable to operate as pure units. Instead, they are the raw material for task-organized, short-term teams that are assembled to deal with a particular tactical situation. Normally this will be something called a "battle group" built upon the assets of the battalion, with artillery, armor, combat and support aviation, and combat-support elements added.

In the Gulf war, infantry was used as essential elements of the combined-arms battle groups. The way this typically works out is for a group to include from one to three tank squadrons (fourteen tanks each), combined with one or two infantry companies (120 men each), plus artillery, engineers, followed immediately with the fuel and ammunition trucks and a multitude of support specialists.

A typical assault will begin with the artillery, traveling behind the tanks and infantry, firing

A lieutenant briefs his platoon before they assault through part of the "Impossible City."

over the heads of the leaders to prepare the objective with a barrage of missiles from the Multiple Launch Rocket System (MLRS) and 155mm fire. The barrage is timed to stop just as the tanks and infantry arrive on the scene, while the defenders are wondering what hit them. The tanks and infantry proceed to finish the job, the tanks dealing with other tanks, the infantry dealing mostly with other infantry. Both will deal with light armor as the opportunity arises. Tanks and infantry both require the services of each other to stay alive.

While the crew of their "battlefield taxi" look on disinterestedly, fire-team members "debuss" an FV510 Warrior. The FV510's 30mm Rarden cannon is effective against lightly armored vehicles at ranges up to about a mile. An entire eight-man section of infantry can be carried. The Warrior provides protection against nuclear, biological and chemical (NBC) agents. It also is equipped with excellent night-vision devices. Each costs about the equivalent of $1 million US. via Will Fowler

Company

British Army companies are commanded by majors, with a captain as second-in-command. There are usually at least three platoons of infantry in such a unit, possibly more or sometimes less. The commander and the headquarters group will ride about in Spartan armored fighting vehicles (AFVs) while the platoons use Warrior AFVs.

Platoon

The platoon is home, sweet home for the soldiers—and kindergarten for the officers. A fresh subaltern, right out of Sandhurst, will be given a platoon as his first command. All the sergeants and soldiers will call him sir, and generally be kind to him, but they won't expect much for a bit; it takes a lot longer than six months to make a fully respectable officer who knows his business. The most important instructor a junior leader can have is his first platoon sergeant; a good sergeant will help the young officer learn all the right moves, develop confidence through competence, learn the art and craft of leadership, and command.

The platoon commander and platoon sergeant work together, with mutually supporting responsibilities. During operations, the officer is responsible for the mission of the platoon, while

A member of the legendary Parachute Regiment sights his SA80. The little four-power telescopic sight is standard equipment although a night sight is fitted to about 10,000 weapons. via Will Fowler

the sergeant is responsible for administration, ammunition, and rations. The platoon commander receives the unit mission, prepares his operational plan and order based on it, and issues the order to the soldiers. The sergeant's business is to ensure that the individual soldiers are prepared mentally and physically, with weapons, supplies, ammunition, and equipment required for the mission.

A bad platoon leader can make life miserable for soldiers in garrison or in the field, and he can get the lot quickly killed in combat. The same goes for the platoon sergeant, although it takes more incompetence on his part to get the whole platoon killed off in one go.

The resources of the typical mechanized infantry platoon include a headquarters element (including the platoon commander, platoon ser-

A company of elderly FV432 APCs charge across the Canadian prairie. The 432 is the technological equivalent of the US M113 APC and is nearly as common in armies around the world. It has been built in numerous variants: mortar carrier, artillery fire direc-

tion center, troop carrier, command post, plus many others. Just as with any other technology, and with people too, they wear out and ultimately need to be replaced. The replacement is the Warrior, which carries two fewer troops but is substantially faster.

A roadblock and vehicle checkpoint in a real-world FIBUA facility. This kind of operation is a common feature of life in Northern Ireland. The mission is to disrupt and deter terrorists. Will Fowler

geant, radio operator, driver, and a runner; all are mounted on an armored infantry fighting vehicle [AIFV or APC] and three sections, each commanded by a corporal, also mounted in AIFVs or APCs.

Section

The individual sections (equivalent to the American squad) are built around two fire teams (Brits call them "bricks"), one led by the section commander (a corporal) the other by the assistant section leader (a lance corporal). Each section gets one light automatic weapon, the LSW, and eight soldiers, plus the vehicle driver.

All the soldiers in the platoon are armed with the Individual Weapon (IW, the basic rifle) or Light Support Weapon (LSW, a squad machine gun).

Of course there are many variations on the basic platoon structure and a plain-vanilla version like this only shows up in text books. Normally the unit will be short a few people, and in training or war, the platoon will probably include visiting sappers, anti-tank gunners, and other temporary guests.

Command and Control

Just how regiments and brigades get used is the so-called art and science of war, the intangible and evasive problem of combat command.

A commander has two fundamental, but conflicting jobs. One is to accomplish a mission, often to engage and destroy another military force. The other part of the job is to preserve the lives and health of his soldiers and their equip-

Foot Guards of 5 Brigade come ashore at San Carlos, Falklands, 2 June 1982, weighed down by heavily loaded rucksacks. Some troops in the Falklands made the long, cross-country approach to the Argentine defended zone under packs that weighed more than 100 pounds—in miserable weather, across sodden, ankle-breaking, wind-scoured tundra. Mechanized transport was virtually nil and all carried heavy loads of ammunition instead of water or rations. Paul Haley/Soldier Magazine

ment. History is full of victorious, acclaimed commanders whose soldiers bought the victory with too many of their lives. That kind of warfighting is no longer acceptable in the United Kingdom or United States, nor in most other modern nations.

British commanders had to win the Gulf war at minimum cost. To do so they had to modify the kind of command procedures they had practiced in Germany, for a different mission against a different enemy on a radically different battlefield than the NATO/BAOR armies had long anticipated.

Brigadier Patrick Cordingley, who led 7 Armoured Brigade in the Gulf, explains it this way:

"When we went on an exercise in Germany, we knew, before hand, what the plan would be. We had been confusing, in Germany, command, and control. We knew in advance where we would withdraw to, where we would refurbish . . . it was *control* the commander was practicing. Never did we get the experience of commanding a really fluid battle—because we just didn't think that sort of thing would happen.

"So, in the Gulf, we quickly came to see that the commander would have to be in a position where he could either see or sense the battle directly, and when there was a problem where he could help, the commander can then communicate forward to his battlegroups, back to his staff.

"This is not the way we've traditionally done things but it has a lot of advantages. But you must give much more scope to your commanders—a certain level of intuition or instinct creeps in as well. Once we've got a mission and understand what our superior's mission will be, we can make our mission analysis more quickly. And, if we are *very* experienced, a certain amount of risk-taking—we absorb the situation and come to an intuitive decision. This allowed me to use a certain amount of native cunning, if you will, that I would have been unable to do had I not had a considerable amount of training.

"The danger here is that, while we are going through the 'appreciation' phase of mission analysis, time is ticking away. If we act very quickly, there is an *opportunity*. If we wait a bit, there is a *problem*. If we wait a long time there could very well be a *crisis*. The better the commander, the more the decision point will move toward the present. Instinct becomes very important and the instinct is the result of training. You've got to train a chap as often as possible under the most realistic conditions, as the Americans have done at the NTC. The NTC recreates those chaotic conditions that are almost impossible to replicate except on the battlefield. It only lacks that final bit of realism, the area where perhaps the British Army is superior, in the area of live-firing exercises where we reduce the safety level and take risks that Americans do not. A combination of the two— the excellence of the NTC and the risks of live-firing—replicate as nearly as possible the pressure put on the commander during decision making."

Brigadier Cordingley elected to fight the battle from a Challenger tank rather than a command and control track as is the usual custom. The drill in Germany has been for commanders to work out of light armored vehicles, normally a FV432, well back in the pack, a procedure Cordingley thinks appropriate for BAOR missions but not for the Gulf's wide-open spaces and rapid movements—and the need for almost instant understanding of the battlefield. He took some criticism for his decision to forgo the big map boards and the accommodations for staff in exchange for the ability to have eyes on the battle, the protection of the Challenger's armor, the thermal sight, the front-row seat. His actions were in the best tradition of battlefield

So-called armored fighting vehicles (AFVs) like the Warrior have become common in the inventories of modern armies only during the last decade or two. The Soviets pioneered the breed with vast fleets of simple, heavily armed designs like the BMP, a hybrid cross between an armored personnel carrier's speed, economy, and capacity, combined with the firepower of a light tank. The Warrior and its American equivalent, the Bradley AFV, don't really have the firepower of a tank, but their 30mm cannons are capable of killing a lot of the light armor on contemporary battlefields.

leadership. And to reinforce them, the brigadier flies the genuine, original Desert Rat pennant that charged across North Africa (and beyond) on the antenna of a succession of 7 Armoured Division command vehicles from 1942 until 1953. It will fly across Iraq and Kuwait, into battle again after a forty-year retirement.

"Now, I wouldn't recommend a tank for everybody" continued Cordingley. "It's incredibly cramped, and you must hope to goodness that you don't have to fire, but you shouldn't be getting yourself in that position anyway. But you're very well protected, you can move as fast as the forward troops.

"The big difference between the American approach and the way we do things is that the

British commander does the mission analysis, does his estimates, makes his plan, comes up with the options and gives them to the staff to work out the details. An American commander does things the other way round—the *staff* will come up with the options and the commander will choose what he believes is the best of them. "So you get a different time scale on the whole thing! The American commander will make a very quick decision . . . but the staff will have worked a very long time on it beforehand. The British commander will take longer to come to a decision because he will have been doing that work himself. So the British commander will be wrapped up in the decision-making process a lot longer than the American commander—which can be a bad or a good thing, but it's a significant difference.

Infantry and armor function as a team, each with its own strengths and weaknesses. The Warrior's infantry section can attack enemy infantry in bunkers, in holes, in buildings where armor can't go. The AFV provides high-volume, long-range firepower, armor effective against most small arms and artillery, NBC protection, night-vision capability, and speedy transport across the terrain.

Infantry in the Gulf War

Three full infantry battalions were sent to the Gulf, with attachments from at least seven others. The units deployed were the 1 Battalion, The Royal Scots (1RS); 3 Battalion, The Royal Regiment of Fusiliers (3RRF); and 1 Battalion, The Staffordshire Regiment (1S). A Coldstream Guards battalion also participated, but only in the dreary business of the care and feeding of POWs in Saudi Arabia.

Infantry Weapons

SA80 Individual Weapon

The basic weapon of the British Army is an odd little device officially called the 5.56mm Individual Weapon (IW), SA80 L85A1. Although it fires the same NATO standard round used by the M16, the similarities begin and end there. It is a small, light weapon with a four-power optical sight as standard equipment. The weapon's barrel and receiver-group are located farther aft than is traditional (a configuration Americans call "bull-pup"), which results in a weapon with the same essentials as a traditional rifle in a package far shorter than the earlier SLR (self-loading rifle) that preceded the SA80. It's only thirty inches long and weighs about eleven pounds with a full thirty-round magazine installed, making it a lot lighter and more compact than the old traditional SLR.

The weapon handles nicely, although the center of gravity sits farther back than for a conventional military rifle. The scope is bright and with a wide field of view; it makes target acquisition and engagement a bit quicker than with open iron sights and a lot faster than with the iron peep sight of an M16—except at very close ranges. The SA80 handles much more like a submachine gun than a conventional military rifle.

The IW, like the older M16 has a selective-fire mechanism that offers single or full-auto fire, the later rated at 610–770 rounds-per-minute cyclic rate of fire. It is supposed to be effective to 500 meters. That's 200 meters farther than the SLR's official rating—and difficult to accept, too, since the old rifle fired the bigger 7.62mm NATO round, which is normally rated at 600-plus

'I'd have gone left flanking myself.'

The English generally have a great fondness for the fauna of the British Isles, even when they become critics of small unit tactics. The specialized art form of military humor probably reaches its zenith in the British Army where a wry, raucous view of life in uniform, with its trials and tribulations, has evolved over many hundreds of years. Kevin Lyles

meters; the difference is probably the result of the IW's scope, which makes it much easier to hit a target at long ranges.

Since it is the standard individual weapon of the realm, the little rifle has replaced the old SLR for ceremonials although it seems horribly unsuited for that kind of drill. It's a bit like trying to drill with a submachine gun—possible, but not satisfying.

Light Support Weapon—LSW L86A1

The LSW is a slightly heavier, beefier version of the IW. It's about four inches longer and two pounds heavier because of extra steel in the barrel and receiver group. The extra metal is to allow the LSW to fire faster, longer than the IW without overheating or wearing out.

In the infantry section, the LSW is replacing the big old General Purpose Machine Gun (GPMG) that has served the British Army so well for so long. The old weapon fires the same 7.62mm NATO cartridge that fed the M60 machine gun as well as the SLR, a good, big bullet with enough power behind it to reach out to 1,000 meters or so with enough kinetic energy left to dent something.

Converting to this smaller, higher velocity cartridge is a bit of a radical change and reflects the diminished role of traditional long-range marksmanship on the modern battlefield. The specifications for the LSW claim an effective range of 900 meters for the weapon as opposed to 800 for the GPMG when used for light support; the older weapon is rated to 1,800 meters (about one mile) when there is somebody able to observe and report the bullet strikes. Although the 5.56mm cartridge has some draw-backs for traditionalists, it has the clear virtue of lighter weight per round, allowing more rounds to be carried.

GPMG

Although displaced from its role as the section machine gun and light support weapon for most British Army units, the old GPMG will stick around for a while longer. In fact, it's an excellent weapon, strong and reliable—and heavy. It weighs about twice as much as the LSW at about thirty pounds (weapon and fifty rounds). Cyclic rate of fire is up to 750 rounds per minute but you can't do that for long before the barrel starts to glow. Sustained rate of fire is 100–200 rounds per minute.

The squad's LSW opens up on snipers firing from an upper story window as a platoon prepares to assault the position. The British soldier's kit is considerably bulkier and heavier than the American equivalent.

The GPMG has been in British service since the 1960s and allegedly has its foundation in the GPMG used by Germany in World War II. It is often used on a tripod, making it far more accurate and effective at long range. The tracers (one in each five rounds in a standard belt of ammunition) burn out at 1,100 meters, limiting the ability of the gunner to spot hits at extreme ranges.

SMG

The little 9mm Sterling submachine gun looks like something left over from World War II, which happens to be essentially true. It's a compact weapon with a pistol cartridge useful in only the most dire circumstances. It is used by truck drivers and people who don't need or have room for a bigger weapon.

With a loaded magazine the weapon weighs about eight pounds. It is rated for 100 rounds per minute. The 9mm round only puts out a muzzle velocity of 390 meters per second—hardly enough to insult some people, much less hurt them. In fact the 9mm parabellum round can be absorbed by the human body in surprising numbers without having much immediate effect on the person's behavior. Of course, after a while they'll probably want to take a couple of aspirin, and perhaps take the rest of the day off, but recovery is quite possible. It is not the first choice of most military people when it comes to knocking down an adversary. Even so it is probably better than issuing the same people handguns; at least the SMG's magazine holds more rounds than does the pistol's.

51mm Light Mortar

The mortar is an ancient weapon, nearly as old as gunpowder. The 51mm version is small and light enough to be taken along by the infantry platoon for those long walks in the country. This little tube, only two inches in diameter, doesn't accommodate a round big enough to do much killing, but nonetheless, it will reach into the nooks and crannies that would otherwise be quite safe from direct-fire weapons. It fires high explosive, illumination, and smoke rounds and has a range of 50–800 meters. At its maximum rate of fire, eight

A member of C Company, 1 Battalion, The Duke of Wellington's Regiment (West Riding) with his LSW version of the 5.56mm Enfield SA80. The regimental tradition provides many British soldiers a kind of professional foundation and historical perspective that is lacking in the US Army. The regiment's successes and failures, both bloody, offer the soldier important lessons in the art of war.

rounds per minute, the supply of ammunition carried by a normal platoon will evaporate very quickly.

81mm Mortar

When the time comes for industrial-strength indirect fire, the British infantry battalion has its own organic supply, the L16A2 81mm mortar. Those extra thirty little millimeters of bore add up to a huge difference in effectiveness, range, and weight. The weapon fires high-explosive

The LSW shares about 80 percent of its parts with the SA80. The LSW has a much greater effective range, though, about 1,000 meters. It is quite light at about thirteen pounds with full thirty-round magazine. Its maximum rate of fire is about 850 rounds per minute, although the sustained rate of fire will be far lower.

(HE), white-phosphorus (WP), and illumination rounds, all out to a range of about 5.5 kilometers or around three miles. This is essentially the same 81mm mortar in service (in modified form) with US Army infantry units.

The 81 is a battalion, rather than company, resource because it and its ammunition are heavy and deserve special attention. Mechanized infantry battalions each include a mortar platoon with four sections, each section operating two 81mm mortars. The weapons, their ammunition, and crews normally travel in either a Warrior AFV or a Land-Rover, but the whole weighty weapon can be split into three major components (barrel, base-plate, and tripod assemblies) that can be carried by dismounted infantry. Such an option is an unpopular one, though, because the whole package weighs in at about sixty pounds ("four stone," say the troops) and each round of ammunition is another ten pounds.

But 81mm ammunition can be worth its weight in gold when the loyal opposition comes up the hill toward your position and the Mortar Fire Controller (an NCO forward observer responsible for fire support coordination) starts calling in 81mm rounds on the advancing enemy. Then each tube can be putting eight rounds of HE and WP on the enemy troops out in the open each minute, if the crews are good. Both rounds have large kill radii, the HE scattering metal shards like little knives and the WP spreading flaming chunks of phosphorus that cause awful burns. Mortar fire is deadly to exposed infantry, dangerous to dug-in enemy, and a damn nuisance to armor.

The 81mm mortar also provides organic fire support for attacks on enemy positions by keeping the defenders' heads down while the attacking force maneuvers toward them. Once the assault force is within a few hundred meters of the objective, the mortar fire will shift to the enemy's suspected fall-back positions.

The mortar's portability has inspired some crafty tactics, one of which is a kind of raid. The mortar section can come screaming up to a preselected firing position with all their firing data already worked out, fire a half-dozen rounds on a target, and pack everything back up and be on the road again before the first round lands. The enemy will try to fire back, but the tormentors will be either out of range or headed in that direction.

Anti-Tank Guided Missiles

Carl Gustav

The Carl Gustav 84 is an old, bazooka-style weapon from Sweden, used by Britain and other NATO nations. It was originally designed as a tank-buster, but modern tanks can shed its projectiles with ease. On the other hand, it will unzip light armor and bunkers like a champ. Normally it is a crew-served weapon, with two soldiers assigned to its care and feeding. It's about a thirty-five-pound package with mount and optical sight, and the rounds each weigh about six pounds. Although scheduled to be replaced long ago, the weapon is still in service

This 7.62mm General Purpose Machine Gun (GPMG) is a German design used by many nations all over the world. It is sturdy, reliable, accurate—and heavy, weighing about twenty-five pounds in the assault, with a belt of fifty rounds dangling from the feed tray. It is effective out to 1,800 meters and can be fired at about 200 rounds per minute until either the enemy assault is defeated or the machine gunner is overrun.

and was used in the Falklands with considerable effect against Argentine bunkers. The Carl Gustav is gradually being replaced by the Hunting LAW80 for light anti-armor duties.

LAW80

The LAW80 is an improved light anti-tank weapon that is alleged to hole armor up to 650mm in thickness. That's about twenty inches—and if the armor were, say, cardboard, that might be accurate; it might even be accurate for plain-vanilla steel, but you aren't going to punch through 650mm of modern frontal tank armor. It is also rated at a range of 500 meters, much better than the old 66mm version, but the LAW80 is much heavier, too, at about twenty-two pounds. The weapon is replacing both the Carl Gustav and the 66mm LAW in the armor, infantry, and mechanized infantry battalions.

Older anti-tank weapons require the gunner to calculate range and target speed before firing through use of fairly complicated procedures. The LAW80 (and its US Army equivalent, the Shoulder Launched Multipurpose Assault Weapon [SMAW]) instead incorporate a little 9mm spotting rifle to make the process a little easier in the heat of the moment. You line up on your target, but before cutting loose with the main event you use the spotting rifle to hit the target. The 9mm rounds are all tracers—you can see them fly down range and hit the dirt above the target; you adjust the point of aim and keep popping away until the tracer pings off the hull of the enemy tank. The little bullet won't really scratch the paint on that T-80 down the hill, but it will tell you exactly where to aim. When you cut the missile loose it will strike in the same spot. This makes the chances of a first-round hit a lot higher than usual, an important factor when you happen to be face-to-face with enemy armor.

Milan

MILAN (Missile d'Infanetrie Leger Antichar) is a Euromissile, designed by Germany and France. It is, like the American Dragon, a man-portable anti-armor weapon with a guidance system that requires the gunner to simply keep the target in the crosshairs during the time of flight, with an electronic system making all the corrections as the missile darts down range. This type of guidance system is called semi-automatic-command-line-of-sight—SACLOS, in the trade. It sounds easier than it is.

But MILAN, even though it is an aging second-generation missile system, has won its spurs and is a mature system thoroughly integrated into the British Army. It is found in all infantry battalions.

Like other TOW (tube-launched, optically-tracked, wire-guided) missiles that have evolved from the Russian Sagger, the MILAN is popped from its launch tube by a gas generator and flies off to its destiny on little wings that pop out after launch. A sustainer rocket motor fires as the missile rips down range, keeping it flying and on course. Hair-thin wires trail out the back, connecting the missile to the control unit in the launcher. The wires create a damn nuisance on the battlefield—they're almost invisible and quite tough and trip up the wandering bands of foot soldiers. But the warhead on the missile is the major nuisance because it is effective against many tanks, vehicles, and fortified positions.

The weapon can engage targets at ranges from 25–2,000 meters. It takes thirteen seconds to reach out to 2,000-meter targets (an eternity on the battlefield) during which time the gunner (who is exposed to hostile fire) must maintain the sight picture perfectly on the center of mass of the target. Hits are not guaranteed.

MILAN is the British equivalent of the US Dragon, another wire-guided SACLOS missile with a medium anti-armor mission. MILAN, though, is far superior to the Dragon in range (double), backblast (none), and firing position (prone instead of sitting). Neither MILAN or Dragon will reliably kill the most modern armor but will melt holes through 350 to 500mm of the conventional steel variety found on tanks like the Soviet-built T-55s, T-62s and T-72s used by many potential adversaries and will take the tracks off anything else. On the occasions when it was used in the Gulf, MILAN cleaned house, scoring twelve hits and kills with thirteen launches. MILAN was used by 2 Para at Goose Green in the Falklands with devastating effect against Argentine bunkers.

Twenty-four launchers are operated by an infantry battalion, each equipped with eight missiles. These are assigned to a dedicated MILAN platoon of four sections, each section having six launchers. During combat operations these sections will be teamed up by the commander and his operations staff with rifle pla-toons, recon elements, or perhaps a mortar team to provide anti-armor support.

Typical of this kind of weapon, the MILAN missile travels leisurely off on its mission at only about 400mph. Newer hyper-velocity weapons and main tank guns are far faster, and time-of-flight on the battlefield is extremely important. A good MILAN section can launch three or four missiles per minute while the ammunition holds out, but they'd better have a lot of good

This cute little 51mm mortar can be fired by one man. Its range is only about a half-mile, but it can deliver specialized fires on the enemy that no other weapon in *the platoon can offer: illumination, indirect high explosive, and smoke rounds.*

Previous page
A Carl Gustav team sets up shop during an exercise. The weapon is now considered obsolete and is being replaced by the LAW.

targets or the sergeant will have a fit; each round costs approximately £9,000 or about US $15,000.

Firing the system is relatively simple. There are two components, the missile (disposable) and the launcher/sight assembly (not disposable). The missile is clipped to the launcher, the electrical connections are made and tested, and the system is armed. The selector is moved to "fire," and the gunner squeezes off a round.

MILAN is used by thirty-six countries around the world, some in combat. According to one report, the system was used in the African nation of Chad to repel a Libyan armored incursion in which more than sixty Russian tanks were destroyed.

Trigat

A third-generation missile, and yet another Euromissile, is a new system called Trigat. The new system uses an infrared beam guidance system rather than the wires on MILAN and the Dragon. It has the same mission, and about the same range as the earlier missiles, but has an improved warhead—and a much costlier price.

Swingfire

The Swingfire missile is a much larger TOW anti-tank missile with some real virtues. It works out to 4,000 meters—a lot farther than a tank gun is usually accurate, offering stand-off advantages. It also allows the gunner to be up to 100 meters from the launcher, another safety enhancement. Control is with a joy stick system that requires the gunner to fly the missile into the target. The missile is used on the AFV438 and the FV102 Striker with cavalry units. Swingfire was used in combat in the Gulf by the 16/5 Lancers.

Aviation

British Army aviation is set up a little differently than its American cousin. The Royal Air Force owns and operates some of the types of systems (the CH-47, for example) that would be US Army property. That kind of arrangement wouldn't be very popular in the United States where the Army and Air Force have very different ideas about missions and responsibilities. But the RAF, by contrast, has dedicated units to support the British Army with troop-lifting helicopters, including the same Boeing Vertol CH-47 Chinook that has been serving the US Army since 1963.

This kind of split loyalties and accountabilities is something American forces avoid at almost any cost. The US Marine Corps, for example, maintains its own little air force of transports, tankers, troop-carrying, and heavy-lift helicopters, plus their own air-superiority fighters (the F/A-18s) and Harrier ground-attack aircraft. These are all organic to the Marines, and the US Army would like to have the same set of organic assets.

While this is not currently the British way of doing things, there is some interest in shifting the 130 RAF troop-lift Chinooks and Pumas to the Army Air Corps (AAC). The AAC operates about 300 helicopters of its own. These are smaller than the RAF helicopters and are used for combat and combat-support missions—as anti-tank gunships and missile platforms, for observation and recon, and for light troop-carrying.

Army aviation units have their own regiments, each of which enjoys a fair amount of individuality. These five regiments include attack squadrons, which currently fly Lynx helicopters armed with TOW missiles, and recon squadrons, which are equipped with Gazelle helicopters. Each of the squadrons will normally operate two flights of six aircraft for each function, attack and recon.

Lynx

The Westland Lynx is a medium helicopter with a multitude of roles: anti-armor (with TOW missiles), troop-carrying, and logistic support, rather like the American AH-60 Black Hawk. Also like other third-generation helicopters of the type, the Lynx has two engines for reserve power and insurance against battle damage, cooling boxes for the exhaust to reduce the exhaust's infra-red (IR) signature, and a combat radius of about 150 miles. Top speed is 175mph.

Twenty-four Lynxes went to the Gulf, none of which were lost in combat. Although not used previously, these aircraft were adapted with sand filters, IR suppressers, GPS, radar-attack-warning (RAW) indicators, and forward-looking-infra-red (FLIR) imaging equipment. This equipment was still not quite up to the ghastly weather conditions during the battle and the planned recon and attack missions for British Army aircraft were mostly scrubbed. Even so, the helicopters provided an anti-armor and flank-protection reserve for the brigade commanders. And on the second day of the war, the Lynx was at least able to demonstrate that its claws and fangs worked.

During the annual NATO Reforger exercise in Germany, a British antiarmor team awaits the "enemy" attack with a MILAN anti-tank missile system, several SA80 rifles, and a Clansman radio, all basic tools of the trade for British infantry. Will Fowler

On G+2, 26 February 1991, 7 Brigade was pushing the Queen's Royal Irish Hussars rapidly forward onto Objective Platinum with two flights of Lynx helicopters from 654 Squadron flying close support. Close support in this case means *really* close, with the aircraft hovering along about fifty feet in the air, just behind the leading edge of the tank formation and traveling at the same slow speed as was the armor. While this is not what anybody ever thought attack helicopters would do in a tank battle, successful warriors tend to be innovators with a tilt toward field-expedient solutions. In other words, if it works, what the hell?

There is a little problem here, however, because a main battle tank's main gun is a terrific weapon to use against helicopters if they are in range. The high-velocity rounds are extremely accurate within range, and the sheet aluminum skin on helicopters is notoriously ineffective at shedding anything that comes out the muzzle of a tank gun. So this low-and-slow approach to the enemy position is asking for trouble, but in this case there were not many options.

The helicopters start launching TOW missiles at extreme range. While the pilot keeps the nose oriented in the general direction of the target, the gunner tracks it with his sight, keeping it in the crosshairs with a small control stick while the missile trails two hair-thin control wires. The maximum range for the missile is about 4,000 meters, with a time of flight of about twelve seconds—a virtual eternity during which the missile bobs and weaves disconcertingly in the viewfinder. The helicopter maneuvers, and the enemy vehicle may also be maneuvering or firing at its tormentors. The first two detonate in the dirt about 100 meters in front of their intended victims, out of range. The second pair of missiles score on enemy APCs, Soviet-built MTLBs. By the time the engagement ends, three APCs and four old Iraqi T-55 tanks are converted to scrap. This is the first anti-armor engagement for British Army helicopters.

Chapter 3

Artillery

British gunners (as they are universally known in all armies) have a reputation for quiet professionalism—except on the battlefield where they are known for extremely *noisy* professionalism. Artillery is an under-appreciated arm, far less glamorous than the dashing infantry or cavalry, but when it comes to killing people and blowing things up, the gunners seem to do most of the work, which is particularly true of the Brits.

In the British Army, artillery is all part of what is called the Royal Regiment of Artillery (RA), about 10 percent of the force. The name is a bit misleading because there are actually twenty-nine regiments in the RA, serving with many kinds of guns in many kinds of roles: with the Paras, as fully Commando-trained gunners with the Royal Marines, as air-defense batteries, counter-battery radar units, field- and heavy-artillery regiments using towed and self-propelled guns, plus a varied menu of missiles to suit almost any taste. It is a complex art and science, the business of lofting a 100-pound projectile across a dozen miles, soaring through space for forty seconds while the earth spins below, winds push and prod above, then to have

Two-pounders in the North African desert—sharp little rat teeth for gnawing on the enemy's tanks and trucks. These little guns were hardly equal to the task of destroying modern armor of the day, but they scored on light armored and light-skinned vehicles. Imperial War Museum

the projectile detonate exactly where it should, when it should. It is an outdoor sport that attracts muscular mathematicians.

Artillery serves several vital functions for the division commander. It offers an organic way for him to deal with threats immediately, without the delay involved in a close-air-support request, out to eighteen miles to flanks or front. The guns can destroy point targets like bunkers, emplaced artillery, command and control facilities like microwave vans or transmitters, all with economy and dispatch. Another kind of artillery, the Multiple Launch Rocket System (MLRS) can spread thousands of little submunitions across a wide area, saturating it with explosive force and fragments, destroying congregations of troops and light vehicles. And when enemy ground-attack aircraft drop in to visit, the air defense batteries greet them with Rapier, Starstreak, and Javelin surface-to-air missiles.

Artillery fits into a British armored division primarily as only one player on the combined-arms team, the big mobile armored brigades that are nearly the size of American divisions. The British armored division includes one component called the Divisional Artillery Group (DAG) to supervise and manage the guns and the gunners at their various tasks. The DAG is commanded by a colonel who, in war, will seldom stray far from the division HQ. From there the assets of the DAG are directed and monitored. The colonel (known officially as Commander

Royal Artillery or CRA) will typically have four regiments to employ, three to provide close support for the maneuver elements, the fourth to fire deep, against distant targets.

Close Support Artillery Regiments

The Close Support regiments field thirty-two 155mm self-propelled (SP) howitzers in four batteries of about eight guns each. These SP

Suffolk gunners from East Anglia man a 5.5-inch gun out on the western desert. Although British tanks and armored tactics were often outclassed by Afrikakorps tanks and tactics during 1941–42, the Germans had *nothing but respect for British artillery forces. British guns and gunners were one of the great success stories of the whole war.* Imperial War Museum

guns look a lot like tanks but have much thinner armor, making them quite vulnerable to almost any anti-tank weapon, including the little throw-away rockets like the LAW. In combat, the SP guns will need to stay behind the lead elements or risk being blown away by any ambitious enemy infantryman. But their extreme range offers tremendous flexibility, with all batteries available to provide mutual support or to mass their fires on one high priority target. Those ninety-six tubes can deliver a tremendous weight of fire on any hapless target that blunders into the path of the advance.

The Close Support artillery regiment fields four Cymbeline counterbattery radar systems to track and plot enemy artillery rounds. Modern technology cuts both ways for military organizations: any advantage you have is probably held by the enemy force as well. As soon as an artillery tube fires it reveals its position and becomes a target itself, either through long-range observation or through any of several ranging/bearing detection technologies, if the enemy is competent, that is.

In the Gulf, for example, this meant that 4 and 7 Armoured Brigades each included one or two tank regiments, one or two mechanized infantry regiments and one artillery regiment as primary combat elements—plus a large cast of supporting players. The artillery batteries get chopped to become elements in task forces assembled for missions designed by the brigade commander, and his operations staff of which the CRA is a part.

Normal British procedure uses four battle groups within the armored brigade. Under normal circumstances each battle group would expect the services of one battery of the AS90 self-propelled guns but normal circumstances are rare in war and the line-up could be quite different, with one battle group getting two—or none, depending on the mission for the brigade, what is actually available to send, and what the threat is across the front.

The battle groups themselves typically include three Combat Teams, smaller task forces with a mix of resources suited to the tactical situation. A Forward Observation Officer (the FOO) for each combat team has eyes on the target to call for fire and provide fire-adjustment instructions. The FOO keeps in close contact with the guns, the fire-support coordinators on the brigade operations staff, and with the regimental fire-direction center.

In the recent past, the forward observer's job required estimates of range, position, and elevation. If he happened to spot a platoon of the opposing force napping out in the open, fat, dumb and happy, he and the battery fire-direction center had to attempt to calculate just where he was and where the target was. The wizards in the fire-direction center would then calculate the range, trajectory, and aiming coordinates and inform the gunners. The gunners would then lay the tubes and fire the mission— and often miss. The target is not likely to sit around cooperatively, though, and will begin looking for holes to hide in or make a dash for some distant refuge. While they're busy doing that, the observer and gunners get to try again, with adjustments. By the time they get the thing right, the target may be gone.

Since about 1970, however, systems like the laser rangefinder have provided far more accurate information for the forward observer. The laser rangefinder and the global positioning system for determining location are stunningly accurate and can describe a target with ten-meter precision. With target data like that, plus the automation of the battery fire-direction center through systems like the British Forward Artillery Computing Equipment (the FACE system), an observer can do what used to be impossible—call "fire for effect!" on the very first round.

Artillery in the Gulf

"I think our artillery was the real battle winner in the Gulf," says Major Andrew Gillespie, O Battery Commander, 2 Field Regiment— the legendary Rocket Troop. "It was quite clear, from interrogations with senior Iraqi commanders, that the air war was terrifying when it started—but after a couple of days they realized that you could hear the airplane coming and, if you got in your hole and were well enough dug in,

after a bit the airplane would go away again. But when the artillery came, it came without warning—and it hit everybody. We hit an Iraqi artillery battery with 250 men in it with MLRS . . . and only eight survived."

Artillery Weapons

FV433 Abbot Self-Propelled Gun

Mounting the excellent but rather small L13A1 105mm gun on an FV430-series chassis for transportation, the Fighting Vehicle (FV) 433 Abbot has been a member of the self-propelled artillery community since the middle 1960s. It is normally accompanied by its faithful squire, the Alvis Stalwart (a six-wheel-drive vehicle) High Mobility Load Carrier, which carts most of the ammunition.

Four men crew the system: commander, gunner, loader, and driver. Their business is to provide artillery support to the armored force in the attack or defense, typically a highly mobile activity. Although the Abbot looks like a tank, it has only thin armor of the same type as used on APCs and only protects the crew against small-arms fire, heavy machine guns, and artillery splinters.

The L13A1 gun fires a full mix of ammunition, including HE (high explosive), HESH (high explosive, squash head—an anti-armor round), smoke, and illumination. It carries forty rounds and can fire twelve of them per minute out to 17,000 meters—about ten miles. The rounds are the same as used in the 105mm Light Gun that serves with British and American units. Unlike the field version, however, the Abbot uses a hydraulic ram to insert the projectile, the powder charge is fed by hand.

AS90 Self-Propelled Gun

The big gun on the British team is the 155mm Artillery System 90 (AS90) self-propelled gun. It is another highly-mobile artillery-support weapon designed to keep up with the armor and to fire over the heads of the attacking force to engage and clear targets that threaten the advance. A typical mission for SP guns involves what American gunners call a hip shoot, a battery rolls into a firing position, executes a fire mission, then moves out again long before the first projectiles arrive on the target.

The AS90 gun is built by Vickers Ship Building and Engineering Ltd, and the barrel can be removed and replaced from the front of the turret in less than an hour. Under dire circumstances the gun can rapid fire at the rate of three rounds in ten seconds—machine gun fire in the artillery department. But six rounds per minute is the fastest normal rate of fire, and then only for brief periods. Normal sustained rate of fire is two rounds per minute.

Forty rounds are stowed aboard the vehicle, twenty-nine in the turret. The gun will fire any 155mm NATO ammunition, and that includes nuclear and rocket-assisted projectiles (RAP). Normally the gun will fire out to 24,700 meters (about fifteen miles), but the extended-range rounds will drop in on a target more than 32,000 meters away, nineteen miles from the gun.

The big six-inch projectile weighs about 100 pounds and enough of that is explosive that even a moderately near miss can throw a tank target over on its back. The projectile meanders leisurely out on its mission at about 800 meters per second, less than one-third the velocity of a main tank round; nearly forty seconds elapse between firing and impact at maximum range.

The AS90 follows the trend in artillery systems development to automate many of the functions of the battery. Using firing data from the battery fire-control party, the gun can be laid automatically and far faster than it could in the previous manual mode. When the SP guns are retrofitted with GPS units, the program to automate the big mobile guns will be even more complete because GPS—when it is working— provides extremely accurate data about the position of the GPS receiver on the surface of the earth. And if a gunner knows exactly where the gun is, everything in range is in first-round danger.

MLRS

The Multiple Launch Rocket System is a big box with twelve large, free-flight (unguided) rockets aboard. The chassis is the same foundation as found on the US Army's Bradley AFV, but with an entirely different turret and cab. It adds an entirely new dimension to the idea of deep artillery fire missions.

Each of those twelve rockets can be fired at a target up to eighteen miles away, far further than any tube artillery firing conventional ammunition. They go where they are pointed with great accuracy, but they are not used against point targets. Instead, MLRS is an *area* weapon

Although it superficially resembles the M109 Self-propelled 155mm howitzer it replaces, the AS90 is a new generation of the breed. It fires the same huge 155mm projectile, available in a wide variety of types (including nuclear). A near miss from one high-explosive round will flip a main battle tank over on its turret. The AS90 has an advanced system called the Turret Control Computer that automates much of the navigation and target engagement procedures to make these tasks more accurate and faster than the previous technologies used by the M109.

that fires against concentrations of vehicles, troops, or anything else of military value. Each rocket dispenses 644 small submunitions, each one of which will destroy a vehicle, including a tank, and will kill troops if it lands within about ten meters of them. The rocket is programmed to dispense these submunitions just high enough above the terrain that they will saturate an area about the size of a football field (British or American variety) with fire. When MLRS fires the whole load of twelve missiles in one awesome ripple-fire barrage, an entire battalion assembly area can be consumed in a shower of smoke, blast, and flame.

Free-flight rockets have been a useful part of the British Army's bag of tricks for several hundred years, ever since Congreve adapted them to military use in the eighteenth century. What makes MLRS important isn't so much the range or the payload but the technology involved in firing the rockets. MLRS uses an extremely accurate navigation system and fire-control computer that permits its crew to download a fire mission from the fire-direction center over the radio, roll up to a firing position, and launch the rockets immediately, without any of the conventional ritual of surveying required for a conventional artillery battery. That gives the commander a resource offering almost instantaneous long-range area firepower to use in emergencies or to exploit an opportunity.

105mm Light Gun

It isn't often that the US Army will buy the weapons of another nation but that's what happened in 1986 with the Royal Ordnance 105mm Light Gun. The US Army needed a new, lighter weapon for the light heli-borne and airborne units that have become essential to modern force projection and held a shoot-out to evaluate all possible contenders. The British 105mm Light Gun won and the US Army bought it because it is a superb bit of engineering that does what artillery is supposed to do—put "steel on target" when needed. With the highly mobile light infantry and airborne units, a compact, durable, accurate, lightweight package is required, and the US Army decided that the Brits

already had a good one. In the United States it has become the M119.

The Light Gun is light enough to be slung under a medium helicopter like the Puma, and in a pinch can be quickly disassembled into two major components and carried by smaller helicopters like the Wessex. It takes half an hour and one wrench to reassemble the barrel and elevating mechanism to the trails. The Light Gun can be towed by just about anything that rolls, including the Land-Rover.

Although it is new to service in the United States, the weapon has been serving in the United Kingdom since its introduction in 1974. The gun fires all the standard NATO rounds, plus a few new ones developed by its manufacturer. The 105mm round is older than dirt, going back to the 1930s, and still accomplishes its mission. It offers a compromise between the mobility of a light gun and the firepower of a heavy one. It is easily the most common artillery caliber on the battlefield.

Standard 105mm rounds will reach out to 17,200 meters, about ten miles, although new extended-range projectiles can add about three miles to that distance. Those projectiles come in a tremendous range of types. The most popular are HE, HESH, WP (white phosphorous smoke/incendiary), marker (colored smoke), illumination, plus several other specialized warheads. American 105mm ammunition can also be fired in the Light Gun although with much shorter maximum range, 11,500 meters being the maximum for a "charge seven" fire mission.

One of these is called DPICM—dual-purpose improved conventional munition—a projectile containing several submunitions that are dispensed over the target. When one of these lands on the vulnerable upper surfaces of an enemy tank, its small shaped-charge will probably cut through the half-inch or so of armored roof and destroy the tank. If it lands on the ground in the vicinity of troops or thin-skinned vehicles, the fragments from the submunitions will cut through their hides as well.

The projectile, fuse, and propellant arrive in separate storage containers, and the gunners have to assemble the rounds before loading. The propellant case contains five small bags of smokeless gunpowder; when the battery fire direction center calls down a fire mission the charge will be specified with the rest of the firing data—charge one means a close-range target and charge seven for one at extreme range, for example. The unneeded bags are removed and destroyed by burning. Then the projectile, with fuse installed and set, is slipped into the brass case, ready for loading.

Antiaircraft Weaponry

Air Defense Artillery

As the poor Iraqi soldiers learned the hard way, tactical airpower and close air support can really put a crimp in the commander's intentions. British soldiers learned the same thing back in the Falklands campaign, among other places.

The bitter lesson (one of many) for the Iraqis was that if you lose control of the skies over your forces it is time to play "let's make a deal." British Jaguars and American A-10s and Apache helicopters were all able to get inside the Iraqi defenses to eat up the enemy forces while staying safely out of range of the weapons available to the other side.

Extremely effective ground-attack aircraft are available to almost any nation. Russia builds several extraordinary models (the agile Su-25 Frogfoot attack jet, the Havoc and Hokum heli-

As cold as it sometimes got in the desert it never got quite as cold as in Norway, where British Army artillery units have frequently trained since World War II. The light gun has been used in combat many times and proved itself during the Falklands campaign where some of the weapons fired over 400 rounds per day. It will fire high-explosive, high-explosive anti-tank, white phosphorus, smoke, and illumination rounds. Maximum range is about ten miles. via Will Fowler

copters) and would like to sell them to just about anybody. Other nations are in the same business. They are cheap (for a combat aircraft), sneaky, and quite effective. If you are a commander of a forward-deployed ground unit the one thing that you have to worry about every minute of every day is the possibility of one of these popping up over the next hill and squirting a few precision-guided munitions into your little camp.

To counter these threats modern armies have mostly discarded the old machine guns that once discouraged low flying aircraft. The Soviet-built ZSU-23-4 (a four-barrel, 23mm antiaircraft machine gun), popular with the Iraqis and many other nations, is the prime example of this and was just about the only thing Iraq had to beat off visiting ground-attack aircraft. Most Coalition aircraft were smart enough (and lucky enough) to stay out of its meager range. They were also able to defeat the relatively slow and stupid shoulder-fired infrared (IR) missiles available to the Iraqis. But if the enemy forces had been better equipped, the complexion and tempo of the war could have been tremendously different.

Starstreak

Starstreak is a weapon that could have created problems for Coalition aircraft had it been used by Iraq. It is a shoulder-launched surface-to-air missile (a larger, vehicle-mounted version is also available), compatible with older generation launchers already in service. It is designed to react almost instantly to the kind of pop-up attacks from low flying jets and helicopters that worked so well in the Gulf through a combination of speed, precision, and an effective warhead.

The missile is tremendously fast, traveling at over Mach 4 out to a range of over seven kilometers (over four miles). Older air defense missiles fly at about one-fourth that speed and to about half that range. It is extremely accurate, with a reported success rate in excess of 95 percent.

The Starstreak's warhead uses three small submunitions, each shaped like the steel dart Armor Piercing Fin Stabilized Discarding Sabot (APFSDS) kinetic energy round fired by main battle tanks. The Starstreak version, though, adds high explosive energy to the kinetic energy for a lethal combination.

There is one tactical problem, though, with advanced-technology weapons like Starstreak: they are so expensive that they become unaffordable despite their marvelous capabilities. Perhaps if Iraq had spent more on weapons of this type rather than on toys like the super gun, the outcome of the conflict might have been different.

Blowpipe

Blowpipe is a much older, more affordable air-defense missile proven in combat in the Falklands—by both sides. It's a shoulder-fired weapon with a 2.4-mile range and Mach 1.5 speed. The missile is guided to its target by the gunner who flies it by radio control. The Argies knocked down three British aircraft with the British-built system—two helicopters, and a Harrier. The Brits outscored the visitors, though, with kills on nine Argentine aircraft (plus two other probables).

Javelin

The new, improved Blowpipe is called Javelin and is replacing the older system gradually. Javelin is faster, at Mach 1.7-plus and has a longer range, out to about four miles. It can be used at night and is easier to use. Javelin is also extremely accurate, with a high success rate during its acceptance testing program. Typically the system is deployed in forward areas where threat warning time is usually brief. There are thirty-six missiles to a Javelin battery within the air defense regiment.

Chapter 4

Armor

After World War II, the politicians and the experts decided that, what with atomic weapons and intercontinental bombers, the services of the infantry and tank forces would no longer be required. There was a sudden restructuring of the military forces of the western world, in Britain and America especially, that cut the size of available forces back to a tiny proportion of their wartime strength and put much of the available resources into air forces rather than land forces. Reality, however, came along to adjust the experts' attitude. In dozens of little backwater conflicts quite inappropriate for the use of bombers, much less atomic weapons, the United Kingdom and the United States both discovered that there still was no substitute for the old, traditional infantry and cavalry. This became especially true in the evolving confrontation between the Warsaw Pact forces and NATO, which, for decades, threatened to become World War III—with or without the nuclear devices. So not all the tanks were melted down right away, and not all the tankers were put out to pasture.

As it turned out, tanks and infantry have been a lot more useful than the nukes. In the Gulf War, armor was the dominant weapon on the battlefield. Iraq used tank forces to invade

A young tank driver from The Queen's Royal Irish Hussars in a rather elderly but still serviceable Chieftain MBT.

Kuwait on 2 August 1990, and it was the combined Coalition armor that chucked them back out in February 1991.

Britain's assignment in the Gulf campaign was among the most challenging and dangerous. The UK 1 Armored Division (there were, confusingly, two "1st Armored Divisions" present on the battlefield—the other was American) was tasked with a sweep up through the very heart of the enemy defenses, along the heavily fortified Wadi al Batin, following the western border of Kuwait to the north and east toward Kuwait City. The new Desert Rats' mission was to fight the bulk of the Republican Guards while the US divisions made their long sweeping end run around the enemy forces from the west. It was a mission executed with some of the best tanks and tank forces fielded by any army anywhere, the product of an appreciation in the United Kingdom, during the last couple of decades, of the importance of the conventional arms.

Send in the Cavalry

The First World War changed cavalry duty. The war began with large, highly trained, and extremely mobile horse cavalry regiments confidently going off to battle. They were slaughtered.

The firepower of the machine gun utterly transformed the business of conflict resolution, beginning about 1914. The need for mobility, for screening and raiding and long-range patrolling

A mixed bag of British armor in North Africa—American Shermans and a Matilda—trundle past some of the wreckage of what had once been a town. Aberdeen Proving Ground

was still present, but the mounted cavalry sent on these missions had an unfortunate tendency to never return. The war became a horrible meat grinder that consumed most of an entire generation of young German, French, Austrian, Belgian, and especially British Commonwealth men—plus a few (by comparison) tens of thousand Americans toward the end. Not many Americans realize that some battles during the First World War consumed more lives in just a day or two than the United States lost in all of ten years of combat in Vietnam. On the first *day* of battle at the Somme, 1 July 1916, the British 4 Army lost 57,000 men, nearly twenty thousand killed. In this one battle alone Britain and France lost half a million soldiers—and it was only one bloody battle of many during a war that very few Americans understand. Battles like the Somme changed the way people thought about war and about fighting wars, and it changed the way we fight them today.

One important change was the introduction of the tank in a highly primitive form. It was about twenty times slower than a horse, but at least machine gun bullets bounced off its hide, most of the time. It was slow, unreliable, awkward . . . and it transformed the battle. However slowly, the early tanks brought movement back to combat and forced both sides to consider new tactics.

Britain took the lead in this reformation. The first effective tanks were British and went into battle in 1916 at Cambrai. The Royal Tank Regiment was formed to develop and use armor during this war, and it still serves. The tank is the principal weapon in the arsenal of the United Kingdom today for land combat, in concert with modern infantry.

The Royal Armoured Corps and Household Cavalry

The British Army includes twenty-four armored regiments, nineteen in the Regulars and five in the Territorial Army. Of the Regulars, two regiments also have special ceremonial duties and are called the Household Cavalry. The Household Cavalry Regiment (Mounted) maintains the old tradition and uniforms of the era of horses in an interesting way. The soldiers who serve in these regiments, The Blues & Royals and The Life Guards, are fully trained, modern tank crewmen who also are fully trained in the gentle art of sitting a horse and ceremonial parades. These duties are alternated in tours of duty that last several months.

Much of Britain's armor is stationed in Germany. Twelve tank regiments there form the 1 British Armoured Corps, along with two armored reconnaissance regiments. Until recently these forces were engaged in the serious business of defending Europe from the Red Horde and were rather welcome. But with the evaporation of the threat comes pressure to get all those big noisy clankers off the street. The British armored regiments' days of tearing up the rural and urban German countryside appear to be numbered, but in the meantime most of the training is done there, although other regiments serve in the United Kingdom and around the world. When the current amalgamations are complete, only six regiments will be left in Germany and two in the United Kingdom, fielding about 550 main battle tanks.

Armor training is done at three principal locations within Great Britain, at Bovington, Catterick, and Tidworth, by Regular regiments that function a bit like the US Army brigades at Fort Irwin, California, (the National Training Center). They are both instructors and adversaries for training purposes, as well as regular combat units with a wartime mission.

British Reserve force elements of the Territorial Army currently field five regiments in the armored-reconnaissance role, two being assigned to support NATO forces in Germany in the event of war, the other three assigned to roaming around the British Isles in their Scimitars and Strikers, defending against the invading horde rather like the horse cavalry of old.

The Armored Regiment

Essentially, two basic kinds of armor regiments are available to the British armored brigade commander: the first being a tank unit—the armored regiment—and the other an armored recon organization—the armored reconnaissance regiment. As with any team, there are two common perspectives for study: from the point of view of the coach or the players. We'll use both.

A tank regiment, in its plain-vanilla form, includes about 600 men, fifty-seven main battle tanks, eight Scorpion AFVs, nine Strike AFVs, plus eight Ferret scout cars. Most of this force is organized into the British tank troop and what Americans refer to as a platoon. There are three tank troops plus an administrative and a medical troop in each tank squadron (the equivalent of a US Army armor company). Four squadrons of main battle tanks, along with a headquarters squadron (for recon, medical support, anti-armor defense, maintenance support) from the regiment.

The tank troops are each equipped with four tanks, each crewed by four tankers. One of these tankers will be a fresh-faced young lieutenant who commands the troop and one of its tanks. The troop sergeant will command one of the others and the remainder are commanded by

Kevin Lyles' rabbits are frequent observers of British Army training, normally appearing in the British Army magazine Soldiers.

corporals. The rest of the sixteen men in the unit are the gunners, drivers, and loader/signalers required by each tank.

The fourteen main battle tanks of each squadron will be commanded by a major, an officer who will certainly know what he is doing. He'll have a tank of his own, as will his number two. His orders will come down from the regiment, usually requiring him to cut and paste elements of his command with elements of other units to assemble task forces for particular missions.

The basic mission for tanks involves a combination of speed and firepower. An armored assault, particularly when executed by a complete regiment (as the Soviets preached in their doctrine) is an entirely awesome experience, from the perspective of both attacker and defender. The speed of each tank, racing across the ground, is amazing. Typically, on suitable ground, the regiment will approach in column, up a road if possible, then be ordered to attack line-abreast. On the desert, the eighty-two tracked armored vehicles will kick up tremendous quantities of dust and may add their own smoke to blind the defenders. About a mile and a half from the defenders, the shooting will begin. Even on the move a modern tank should kill its target with the first shot at 2,000 meters.

The attacking regiment will typically rely on the overwhelming, intimidating shock of its massed bulk, speed, and fire. Some of the attackers may (and against a competent defender a great many will) be destroyed while making their assault. But if the attacker is competent, the defenders will find themselves task-saturated, overwhelmed by one target after another. Sooner or later the defenders will die or will begin to consider their options. If the attack isn't stopped, the defenses will be gradually ground away—*attrited* is the military term—until the survivors either run or surrender or are killed off. On the other hand, a good defense can grind down the attackers until they are worn down to nothing. A few attackers might even survive long enough to reach their objective, although that could be a hollow victory.

Inside the tanks of both defender and attacker, the crews work with electric intensity, each on an adrenaline high. The commanders and gunners search for targets through the smoke and dust. Through their sights they may (or may not) spot the flash from the main guns of the hidden defenders, revealing the defense's position. The commanders and gunners won't notice, usually, the many hidden anti-tank-missile positions emplaced around the defensive position.

The commander will normally identify the target, designate it, and issue the fire command, although the gunner can engage on his own. Either way, it is identified, an ammunition type called for, and engaged, all within less than a second or two. "TARGET!" yells the commander. "T-72 . . . Sabot . . . "

The commander will traverse the turret quickly to the target, find it in his sight, hand it off to the gunner who acquires it, aligns the gun on the target center-of-mass, and makes sure the fire-control computer is programmed for the selected ammunition—APFSDS.

The loader will select the ammunition the commander or gunner wants; for a main battle tank, ammunition will usually be a kinetic energy round, a long, thin, heavy dart made of tungsten steel or depleted-uranium alloy. It is far smaller than the gun tube so the dart is surrounded by a sabot that will fall away immediately after the projectile leaves the muzzle. In a swift, practiced move, the loader removes the projectile from a storage bin, inserts it into the breech, and rams it home with a hydraulic ram. Then the propellant case is selected, extracted, and slid into the breech; the breech block slams closed with a *thunk*. This process takes about two seconds, start to finish. "Up!" reports the loader.

The gunner finds the target in his primary sight, centers it, enters the ammunition data in the fire-control computer, and prepares to fire. Although the tank is thrashing across the rugged terrain, pitching and rolling, the image in the gunsight is stable with the crosshairs on the center of mass. And, from the outside of the tank, the gun tube is locked on the target, stabilized, and isolated from the movement of the tank. When the gunner is confident about his firing solution and the commander has given the firing order, the gunner calls "On the way!" and fires.

When the main gun fires, an observer outside sees a fireball about twenty feet across flash in front of the vehicle, the blast raising dust all around the vehicle, the noise deafening, even a kilometer away. If the tank has been hiding in a hole in the battlefield, it is no longer hidden—everyone now knows where it is.

From inside, not much happens; the crew feels a mild jolt, hears a gentle thump. The gunner's view of the target is momentarily obscured by the hot gasses of the burned propellant. The projectile appears in the sight, a glowing dot streaking downrange toward its prey at about one mile per second.

When the projectile strikes (and it will about 90 percent of the time), the slender rod of heavy alloy retains a tremendous amount of kinetic energy, enough to turn the projectile and the armor that it contacts into white-hot liquid. In milliseconds it will melt a hole through about a foot and a half of armor, and then molten material sprays the contents of the target.

Two things typically happen then: one is that the tank catches fire gradually, over about fifteen seconds—"brewing up" the Brits call it. The hydraulic fluid, propellant for the main gun rounds, smoke grenades, or perhaps the fuel for the engine will light first. The tank may continue to blunder across the landscape but smoke and flame will start to show from under the turret ring or perhaps from the hatches. Occasionally crew members will bail out of the tank, if they are lucky. When the fire reaches the propellant for the main guns, though, the effect is suddenly like that of an immense blow-torch being ignited inside—jets of intense flame blast from the turret hatches and other openings.

The other alternative is even more dramatic. The propellant and the high-explosive projectiles stowed in the target actually detonate rather than just burn. When that happens, the turret (weighing many tons) will shoot up into the air for about fifty feet, sometimes with the commander still poking out his hatch, as was witnessed in the Gulf. It is an impressive sight, and a sobering one.

Tankers know that they are targets and that such a fate awaits the unwary, the unlucky, and the inept. It can happen to anyone on the battlefield, friend or foe alike. So to improve the odds as well as get the job done, tactics have been developed to use armor in combat most effectively and efficiently.

Tank Tactics

The tanks, and even the troop, will seldom be asked to operate independently. That's just as well because the lieutenant probably still has a lot to learn. It is also because a tank troop can get into a lot of trouble by itself, even with the best of commanders. It takes a combination of

The Challenger 2 main battle tank designed for the British Army by Vickers Defence Systems. Challenger actually started out as a project for the Iranian armed forces but after the Shah was deposed the contract was canceled. The design was adopted and adapted by the British Army and has turned into a tremendous success. It has a crew of four and carries forty-four rounds for the main gun plus 6,000 for the machine guns. via Will Fowler

tanks and infantry, with artillery support and combat engineers on call, to cope with most missions.

Tanks can defend or attack. They do both well, and both badly, depending on who's doing what to whom. They are traditionally the premier anti-tank weapon. In defense a tank can worm its way into the ground until nothing shows from the front but the top of the turret. In fact, a good defensive position will be dug so that, from two miles away the only thing exposed is the commander himself, peering out across the landscape through binoculars, essentially invisible to another tank approaching. When the enemy tank gets in range, the defender drives forward about twenty feet, up a ramp that has been carefully crafted by the engineers, exposing the gun tube and turret while keeping the rest of the hull safely hidden behind a thick earth berm. Even if the enemy tank, now two kilometers away, spots the defender and attempts to engage with his own gun, the odds are unequal because the enemy is fully exposed in the open while the defender shows only a bit of the turret. It seems an unfair contest, and it is—if there are just two tanks involved.

There are almost never two tanks involved. Instead, there is the whole combined-arms mix of aviation, artillery, infantry, and special forces fighting the defensive and the offensive battle together. The attacking enemy avoids blundering into such situations by using all kinds of reconnaissance, from the air and ground, to discover where the defenders will be. And if such a well-prepared defender must be confronted head-on, there are ways to make these immobilized tanks suddenly exposed and vulnerable.

One way is to use artillery and aircraft to dispense thousands of little submunitions across the terrain occupied by the defender, saturating these positions with small shaped charges that will blast through the thin roof armor of even the most modern main battle tank. Another is to use ground-support helicopters and fixed-wing aircraft to nail the defenders in their holes, with precision missiles or area weapons. Even if the defenders elect to make a break for the border, artillery and aircraft can spread mines across wide areas of the enemy route of march, slowing, attritting, and possibly stopping them.

A common mission for a tank-mechanized infantry team is to clear an enemy position. This could be a bunker or trench complex, an airfield, or a village. For tanks alone, these places are deadly dangerous, full of little hiding places for enemy anti-tank gunners with wire-guided missiles or even camouflaged direct-fire artillery. The enemy can pop up from anywhere and squirt a TOW missile at the visiting team.

To defend against such a problem, the infantry squaddies debuss from their APCs and work through the enemy position on foot, clearing the bunker complex (for example) with rifles and grenades. If an enemy elects to fire on the infantry, he immediately becomes a target for the infantry weapons, plus the tank's main gun or coaxial machine gun. Artillery and close air support can be called in.

The artillery is a crucial element. It is self-propelled—either the old Abbot, with a 105mm gun, the American designed M109, or the British designed AS90. These guns are all as mobile as the tanks, and move with, but behind, the tanks. The tanks are able to provide extremely accurate direct fire out to, at the most, three miles—the immediate threats. The artillery, though, provide indirect, high-angle fire that is accurate out to more than ten miles, with huge projectiles that weigh 100 pounds. The long range and heavy weight of fire offered by modern 155mm artillery give the task force commander tremendous flexibility in the defense and the assault.

Artillery is usually (not always) a stand-off weapon that will out-range its target. A tank, for example, can't engage the 155mm howitzer firing at it from the other side of the mountain. Another crucial stand-off weapon system that was frequently decisive in the Gulf War was the attack helicopter with missiles that easily out-range tank guns.

Within this mixture of attackers and defenders are a very few unarmored, nearly unarmed, yet extremely dangerous weapons systems—the special forces soldiers hidden in their holes, watching and reporting back to the task force commander's staff. They may be SAS teams, dug into hides so perfect that you can stand on top of one and not know a British soldier is within knife-fighting range. The observer will normally never confront an enemy, fire a shot, or be revealed to the opposing team, and yet he can be responsible for the death and destruction of battalions and brigades. He does this with three weapons systems, plus experience, training, and judgment.

The weapons are called GPS (Global Positioning System), digital message transmission system, and the laser rangefinder. With these, the observer can describe the exact location of a target with a very short burst of encoded information over the radio. The burst transmission makes it much more difficult for the enemy's electronic-warfare systems to detect and identify the observer's location (although it can certainly be done).

A detachment of Royal Hussars from 1 Armoured Division, British Army of the Rhine (BAOR), on exercise with the Challenger 1. The Challenger 1 has a four-man crew, a 120mm gun and a Rolls Royce 1,200hp diesel engine that can propel the vehicle up to about 35mph. The armor is of the Chobham laminate type, able to resist most modern anti-armor projectiles. via Will Fowler

The Battle Plan

Using all these resources, plus many others, the commander and his staff plan their battles and issue a plan that is extremely flexible. That plan is called an *order,* but it is not something that normally must be slavishly obeyed to the death. Instead, the order is a detailed guide that the whole battle group will use to coordinate their efforts. It will include general information such as the mission, the threat, the resources committed, and support available. It also includes detailed information that will be important to coordinate the hundreds of people involved: radio frequencies, coordination times for artillery prep fires, times to start moving, and when and where to stop. Much of the information will be placed on maps marked with phase lines and boundaries that help with the coordination of these vast fleets of tanks and other weapons. There are two extremely important graphics added to the map overlays: the objective and the line of departure.

The brigade commander and his staff issue the operation order to the regimental commanders, who go back to their regiments and add their own details and then issue the order to

the squadron commanders. The majors go back to the squadrons, gather the lieutenants and issue their version of the order. The troop commanders dutifully copy everything down, go back to the troops and gather up the squaddies for a chat. Everybody has an assignment. Each commander—from the corporals commanding tanks on up—has a map, a lot of notes, an idea of the commander's intent, and a pretty good idea of what his little role in the big extravaganza is supposed to be, who he is responsible for, and who he is accountable to.

Now, if that sounds like a recipe for disaster, you're right. One of the grand traditions of all military units is that confusion reigns supreme, particularly at moments of crisis. It is the reason why British soldiers train constantly, why everybody goes through the motions a thousand times out on the Salisbury Plain and on the German training ranges before going to war. British soldiers train the way they expect to fight, with intensity and attention to detail. Wellington said that Napoleon's marshals made plans like beautiful pieces of fitted harness, but if the unexpected happened, they were done for—while his own plans were like bits of rope. If one broke he could tie a knot and carry on. And that's the way British commanders still design their plans.

Armor Weapons

The lance, bow, and sabre of the past have evolved over the years to muzzle-loading muskets and smooth-bore artillery, to rifles and high velocity artillery, from horses to early armor, to today's amazing main battle tanks like the marvelous Challenger. Impervious to almost all anti-armor projectiles from other tanks, able to destroy virtually anything else on the battlefield, this remarkable, costly, complicated weapon system is the leading edge of technology—for the moment.

FV4030/4 Challenger Main Battle Tank

The Fighting Vehicle 4030/4 (FV4030/4) Challenger is Britain's most modern main battle tank, which, considering that the United Kingdom has traditionally produced some extremely innovative and effective tanks, is important. The tank in service today is an evolution of the older Chieftain tank, which has been around since the 1950s. The Challenger was originally intended for export sales to Iran and called the Shir 2, but the project was adopted by the British Army when the Shah was overthrown and when a Eurotank project involving British and German army requirements fell apart. It is manufactured by the Royal Ordnance factory at Leeds; about 450 have been delivered since the design entered service in 1983.

The Challenger's main gun is a rifled 120mm L11A7, a fully stabilized system with an advanced fire-control system. Laser range finding, wind sensor, barrel wear- and warp-sensors are all part of the Integrated Fire Control System; within range, the Challenger will normally score a hit with the first shot out of the tube,

Tank commander (left) and loader/signaler (right) try to keep up with the tactical plan. British tankers have been helping to tear up the German countryside for *nearly fifty years, first in pursuit of the Nazis, then during NATO maneuvers.* via Will Fowler

regardless of whether the Challenger or its target are moving or not. The tank carries a supply of kinetic-energy rounds and high-explosive projectiles, along with a few smoke rounds, in an ammunition locker in the turret.

The tank is also armed with two 7.62mm machine guns, primarily for use against enemy dismounted troops, plus smoke-grenade launchers that can screen the tank from enemy gunners. According to the published specifications, the Challenger is good for about 36mph on the road—but 50-plus is more likely. Power comes from a Rolls-Royce Condor V-12 diesel engine developing 1,200hp.

The Challenger's turret and hull are protected with the Chobham composite armor developed by the British and used on the US Army's M1 Abrams tank. This material, details of which remain highly classified, is a laminate of ceramic materials, titanium alloy, and mesh that effectively counters both shaped-charge antitank warheads (TOW missiles, HEAT (High-Explosive Anti-Tank) rounds from other tanks) and the kinetic-energy projectiles that are now the first choice in anti-armor weapons. The layers effectively disrupt the jet of super heated gas formed by the shaped-charge warhead, diffusing its effect.

The Challenger 1s are going to be up-gunned with the L30 CHARM 120mm gun and an improved commander's cupola that will allow a commander to acquire and designate targets directly for the gunner to engage.

Four men crew a Challenger, and just about every other modern main battle tank (although the Russian designs use three). The tank commander will be an officer or NCO, responsible for what the tank does, and the other three support him. The commander sits or stands in position on the right side of the turret. His seat is adjustable, allowing him to stand with head and shoulders outside or sit, with the hatch battened down. The first position offers far better visibility, an extremely important element of the commander's job because, as in most forms of combat, the first to fire is going to be the survivor. But standing in the hatch in a combat environment is also dangerous as hell; artillery

Armor units do their large-scale exercises in Canada where there is plenty of room for the regiments to frolic. The frolicking can go on for days without rest. When at last the exercise is over everybody feels like a combat casualty. This exhausted crewman is waiting for his turn at the wash rack where the vehicle will have a bath, then he will get a chance to visit the "personnel wash rack" for the first time in perhaps a week. via Will Fowler

can burst overhead at anytime, and enemy snipers will be praying for the moment that a tank column drives by with the commanders exposed. The Challenger, particularly the Mk2 with the new Active Cupola Target Acquisition System (ACTAS), give the commander sufficient visibility to deal with the kind of threat Iraq offered with good security, but against a really modern, skilled force the odds would be much worse.

To the commander's left, behind the gun, is the loader/signaler. This is the most junior position on the crew, an entry-level position for the novice tanker. While it doesn't require a lot of experience, it does demand considerable strength and agility to manage those big 120mm main-gun rounds within the tight confines of the turret. This task is harder than it sounds, and it is *very* poor form for the loader to stick the commander with the needle point of the kinetic-energy round while trying to maneuver it into the gun.

But the loader's job in a Challenger is a bit more complicated than his American counterpart's in the M1A1 Abrams. Instead of one big round to wrestle with, the Brit loader loads the projectile and the propellant cases separately into the gun. The projectile can still be a weighty issue—up to about thirty-five pounds for some types—but the physical size of the round is much more manageable.

The rounds themselves are rather interesting, too; instead of the old metal cartridge cases that once piled up in the turret, the new 120mm ammunition uses combustible cases that reduce the trash problem in the tank to almost nil. They are stored under the turret ring in the hull of the tank, each round fitting into its own protected little pantry. These individual ammunition stowage lockers are surrounded by a flame suppressant and the more recent Challengers have extra armor for the ammunition stowage lockers. Sixty-four projectiles can be stowed aboard the tank, along with forty-four containers for propellant cases.

The mix of ammunition types available for combat include APFSDS (Armor-Piercing Discarding-Sabot), and HESH (High-Explosive Squash-Head). Of these, the choice against most armored targets will be the APFSDS.

Besides feeding the main gun, the loader manages the radios, and when not otherwise occupied serves as lookout with a one-power periscope mounted in his hatch and fetches tea for his mates.

The gunner sits in front of and lower than the commander, on the right side of the turret, squeezed in to an extremely confined station beside the main gun. The gunner's job is the essence of the tank's mission; he puts the steel (or depleted uranium) on the target. He is expected to hit an enemy tank, on the move, in darkness, with blowing smoke and dust, without fail at ranges of about a mile—with the first shot. That first shot will probably have to be made within five seconds from the time the commander or the gunner identifies the target. Within that five seconds the gun must be loaded

Challenger 1 on maneuvers in Germany. The tank is protected by Chobham armor, a complex and exotic material that is believed to include multiple layers of ceramics, titanium alloy, and nylon mesh and that is supposed to protect against virtually all anti-tank missiles and projectiles. The Challenger 1 is fitted with the 120mm L11A7 gun. The powerplant is a conventional diesel built by Rolls-Royce, producing 1,200 hp. Will Fowler

with an appropriate projectile and propellant case; the gun tube brought to bear on the target; the fire-control computer programmed with range, ammunition type, and atmospheric conditions; and the cross-hairs aligned on the target center-of-mass. During this time the Challenger is probably moving, and the target may be preparing to fire back.

Advanced technology makes the gunner's job more efficient and effective by integrating the gun tube, the drivetrain that points the gun, and the sighting system. The gunner's primary sight is the Thermal Observation and Gunnery System (TOGS) that has one-power and ten-power magnification choices with an 8.5-degree field of view. Integrated into the sight and fire-control system is a laser rangefinder that provides accurate data out to 10,000 meters (six miles) and is extremely accurate under 3,000 meters.

The driver sits up forward in the hull where he drives the tank with controls rather like those of any conventional car or truck. The transmission is automatic, with forward and reverse gears driving the huge tracks on the vehicle.

The powerpack is designed for quick changes and can be extracted in the field in less than an hour. Such changes are fairly common because it's easier and faster to simply swap out a powerpack that is having problems and pop in a fully functional one to get the tank back to the battle.

The whole drivetrain for any tank is an engineering challenge. The vehicle weighs over 100,000 pounds, travels across open country, over ditches, through streams, and occasionally on roads. It needs to be able to turn on a shilling, accelerate and brake rapidly, and still have fuel economy that allows practical operation.

At £2 million (1987 prices) per copy, the Challenger is luxury transportation. More than 400 have been delivered and are in service in the tank role, along with over seventy variants serving as armored repair and recovery vehicles (ARRVs). The ARRV dispenses with the main gun and adds a crane capable of extracting the Challenger power pack and a bulldozer-type blade.

FV101 Scorpion Light Tank

Main battle tanks are too expensive, bulky, and available in too few numbers to be used for all the missions that need to be accomplished. For these reasons, all modern armies supplement their heavy armor with large fleets of lighter, less expensive vehicles like the Scorpion.

Officially, it is the Fighting Vehicle 101 (FV101). It uses aluminum armor, is run by a crew of three, and is powered by a Jaguar XK 4.2 engine. The whole package weighs in at about 15 percent of the Challenger's weight. It zips around the battlefield faster than the Challenger at 50mph and will range out to about 380 miles. It's armed with a 76mm gun and a 7.62mm machine gun, and carries forty rounds of the big stuff and 3,000 for the machine gun. The 76mm gun will reach out to 5,000 meters—three miles.

The FV101 has the great virtue of being small enough that two fit inside a C-130 Hercules, the ubiquitous aerial delivery truck used by the United Kingdom and many other nations. It has an advanced thermal sight system and laser rangefinder and is undergoing upgrades for the gun and powerpack that will provide extra range in both departments. New models should be able to get over 1,000 kilometers on a tank of gas—600-plus miles.

Like other light armor vehicles, the Scorpion is fairly easily squashed. The light armor will keep out small-arms fire and artillery fragments, but an anti-armor round from anybody on the battlefield will disassemble the Scorpion and its crew into their component parts. Main-gun rounds of the kinetic-energy type will slice through that thin armor like it was soft cheese. So the Scorpion relies on speed, stealth, and an alert crew to avoid threats—and they let the big Challenger lead the way whenever they can.

Scorpion's mission is reconnaissance—sneaking around the front or the flanks of the main body of the force, keeping an eye on the enemy, or places the enemy might use. The Scorpion's weapons, like those on other light armor vehicles, aren't an excuse to go out and take on enemy heavy armor, but to serve as self-

The wee little Ferret scout car looks a bit like a relic from World War II—and so it is, an update of the old Daimler scout car that prowled the desert with the original pack of Rats. It is still well liked and extensively used by the British Army for all sorts of reconnaissance and liaison roles. The Ferret has a crew of two or three. The Mark 4 version (shown) has a simple .30-caliber machine gun for armament while the Mark 5 gets a rack of four Swingfire missiles bolted to the turret. It can achieve about 50mph on roads. Michael Green

defense weapons when there is no choice. A recon vehicle's best armor is plenty of distance between itself and the folks shooting at it, preferably with a big hill in between. But for those chance encounters, particularly where the opposing force is snoozing, disabled, alone, or too close to avoid, the 76mm gun will probably be effective against older-generation tanks such as the Soviet T-62 and earlier, and maybe against the more modern T-72s. The thermal sight will help in such an engagement because few of the older Soviet-supplied tanks have good night vision gear or infra-red sensor systems.

FV102 Striker AFV

The Striker is another recon vehicle, a close relative of the Scorpion, with thin armor and plenty of speed. But instead of running from enemy armor, the Striker is supposed to stand and fight—if the tactical situation permits—with its Swingfire TOW missiles. Since Swingfire can out-range most tank guns, this works well enough for ambushes in open terrain. But if enemy armor gets within their own effective gun range (about one to two kilometers), the Striker has a problem.

FV432 APC

The basic battlefield taxi for British soldiers is the Fighting Vehicle 432 (FV432), an armored personnel carrier similar to the M113 still used by the US Army. Like the M113, the vehicle has been around a while, and most of the 2,300 in service are beginning to wear a bit thin in spots. Its principal role from the beginning, back in 1962 when it was introduced, was to shuttle troops around with speed and comfort. The speed and comfort are relative, however, to walking and being exposed to small arms and artillery fire. The dear old 432 is far slower than the Warrior APC, its replacement in the inventory.

The FV432 provides the foundation for many battlefield duties including the task of carrying around the L16 81mm mortar and its crew, and it allows them to fire from within its lightly armored confines. There is plenty of room for the big tube and plenty of ammunition—160 rounds of HE, smoke, and illumination. The mortar itself is mounted on a turntable that permits the weapon to fire in any direction relative to the chassis of the vehicle, launching rounds out to a maximum range of three miles. In this configuration, the FV432 uses a crew of six.

It also carries the Cymbeline counterbattery radar used to locate enemy mortar teams firing on friendly units. Such systems make the life of the mortar teams easier because they detect incoming artillery rounds in flight and are able to plot the trajectory of the rounds right back to the little spot on the battlefield from which they were launched. That little hiding place then becomes a target for any artillery battery in range. Cymbeline has a range of 20,000 kilometers—twelve miles.

The FV432 also serves as recovery vehicle, mine layer, maintenance support, command track, Carl Gustav and MILAN carrier, and ambulance.

Unlike many APCs, the FV432 uses all-steel armor. The driver sits in the forward part of the hull, with the track commander farther aft in his own little turret. The commander has a 7.62mm GPMG or the Bren 7.62mm LMG installed for close encounters with enemy dismounted infantry, but this is not a tank, and mixing it up with any sizable force is strongly discouraged.

The FV432 has a nuclear, biological, and chemical (NBC) system that reduces risk to the crew and passengers from exterior nuclear radiation or biological and chemical weapons and is airtight in that respect at least. It isn't watertight, however, and must be prepared for stream crossings deeper than fording depth.

A Rolls-Royce K60 engine provides 240hp for the FV432 and can push it up to about 35mph. This engine is a straight six-cylinder version without turbocharging. Like many vehicles of

A Challenger 1 deep in the heart of Germany trains to defeat the Red Horde. When push came to shove, however, the battlefield didn't look a thing like the northern European scenario that everybody had trained for. Instead, it was the same kind of battlefield that *confronted the first generation of Rats a half a century earlier—and the Rats again prevailed. They fought against the same Soviet-designed and built tanks and tactics for which they had trained.* Will Fowler

this type, it uses just about any fuel that happens to be handy—gasoline, diesel, and maybe even vodka. A semi-automatic transmission is linked to the forward drive sprockets providing six forward gears, reverse, and steering control.

FV510 Warrior APC

Warrior is the name given the latest generation British APC, the Fighting Vehicle 510 (FV510), intended to replace the FV432 over time. The design was accepted in 1984 and began serving with the British Army in 1988. Approximately one thousand are on order with 400 in service at this writing, and the rest are to be delivered by 1995.

The Warrior is smaller inside and bigger outside than the faithful old 432, but faster and with a bigger punch. You can wind it up to 75kph—about 45mph—and blast away at the enemy with a Rarden 30mm cannon instead of the little 7.62mm GPMG.

The Rarden cannon is good for about a mile and will punch holes in armored personnel carriers and fighting vehicles like the ubiquitous Soviet BMPs and BRDMs, built and sold by the thousands. The 30mm cannon is housed in a two-man turret with full power controls and one-power and eight-power day and night sights. The Warrior is more useful on the battlefield than its predecessor and more able to mix it up with certain adversaries—but it is still no match for a tank made after 1970. Aluminum is used for the armor and is supposed to be more effective than the steel used in the FV432.

It will cross an eight-foot ditch without falling in and getting stuck (usually) and can climb a 60 percent slope. It will also go up a two-and-one-half-foot wall if necessary, although it is hard on the tracks.

Its road range is less, at about 300 miles on a tank of diesel. It accommodates eight infantrymen (a full infantry section) instead of ten. Power comes from a 550 horsepower Rolls-Royce CV8 engine that feeds the front sprockets through an automatic transmission with four gears. If you stomp on the gas, the result isn't exactly "patching rubber" but acceleration is brisk for the 50,000-pound sports car class: 0–50km/h in only eighteen seconds. Such acceleration cuts into the fuel economy, however, so don't expect to get the 2.5mpg (highway) consumption that the careful driver can expect.

Typical of APCs everywhere, the Warrior shows up in a variety of forms, including command-and-control vehicles, artillery spotters, and repair/recovery vehicles.

The manufacturer will tell you a Warrior can accommodate its crew of three, plus eight infantry soldiers, for forty-eight hours of nonstop battlefield activity, but they don't tell you what it will smell like after a day or two or whether any of this lot will be speaking to each other.

FV721 Fox Light Armored Car

While most armored vehicles on the battlefield are huge, ponderous beasts that can scarcely get out of their own way, there is one, a little British battlefield sports car, that is super fast, corners like a maniac, gets great gas mileage (in its class), and is just the thing for a rally or a little drive in the country. And if the competition gets tough, it can literally blow them away.

The little Fighting Vehicle 721 (FV721) Fox is a direct descendant of the small, wheeled, light armored Daimler scout cars that patrolled the North African desert during World War II, and the Daimler's offspring, the Ferret scout car from the 1950s. The World War II version rambled all over the desert, keeping tabs on Rommel while trying to stay out of range of the guns of the Afrikakorps. The current generation is a product of the 1960s and has been in service since 1973 with both the Regular Army and the Territorial Army, but it still looks like its grandparent. Despite an old and obsolete impression, it's a handy and modern little thing, with much work to do in the British reconnaissance regiment.

The Brits and other European armies have long appreciated the virtues of wheeled vehicles on the battlefield and have consistently included them in the stable of armor. They are fast, light, uncomplicated, and reliable. The Fox uses the 195hp Jaguar J60 gasoline engine with electronic ignition, a unit that propels the beast to more than 60mph. All four wheels are powered through a five-speed automatic transmission that ultimately drives those four huge 11x20 "run flat" tires. The hull is welded aluminum, thick enough to stop small-arms fire and artillery fragments. Inside is enough room for three tourists—a driver, a commander, and a gunner.

The little Fox has big teeth; a 30mm Rarden cannon with ninety-nine rounds can deal with light armor, and a 7.62mm machine gun is available for infantry targets. A thermal sight is available for night use. Variants include models with other gun systems and the MILAN missile launcher.

The basic mission for the Fox is recon—snooping on the loyal opposition and staying out of trouble if possible. It is small and light enough to deploy with just about any unit; three will fit into a C-130, and two can be dropped as a single parachute load.

Signals and Electronic-Warfare Systems

Clansman

The Clansman family of radios is used throughout the British Army for communications at the tactical level. Eight systems are available, from the little PRC-349 carried by every infantry squad to the powerful VRC-321 installed in tanks and other vehicles. These radios are all high-frequency (HF) or very high-frequency (VHF) systems normally used for voice communications between ground units. Some of these Clansman systems allow communication with British air and sea units as well.

Wavell

Wavell is the commanders' battlefield computer used for some battle-management functions. It is a big, heavy, expensive piece of gear that rides around in its own armored personnel carrier, attended by a small staff of specialists. It is a brigade asset, used to integrate information from the many reporters supplying information to the commander's staff. It is, essentially, a mainframe computer on tracks—not exactly a laptop, but it will go just about anywhere, and the batteries don't quit after a couple of hours' use.

Chapter 5

Rats in the Gulf

SitRep: 0001 Hours 24 February 1991

On the cold, damp, dark morning of 24 February, the months of waiting for the new Desert Rats were finally over. For Brigadier Patrick Cordingley and his 7 Armoured Brigade, the orders and the waiting had begun back in the remote German town of Soltau in mid-September. Number 7 Brigade is a tank unit, equipped with the latest Challenger MBT, the most suitable unit for British deployment.

Number 4 Armoured Brigade followed, with Brigadier Christopher Hammerbeck commanding. It is an infantry-heavy organization—highly mobile, extensively trained, well-equipped—and the perfect partner for the tankers of Cordingley's brigade.

The two units combine as the core of a modern armored division, formed for the occasion and called 1 (British) Armoured Division, with Major General Rupert Smith the GOC (general officer commanding). The official emblem for what will henceforth be universally known as *1 Div* is a white rhino, but the creature's parents are two North African rodents, one black and

the other red, and unofficially the whole bloody lot are called the Desert Rats.

Above them all on the chain of command are the theater commanders, Lieutenant General Sir Peter de la Billière (Commander, British Forces Middle East) and Air Chief Marshal Sir Patrick Hine (Joint Commander, British Forces Middle East). They report to the Chief of the Defense Staff, Marshal of the Air Force Sir David Craig. He reports to (as far as the troops are concerned) God.

General Smith and the other senior commanders are a new breed. World War II British commanders, while not exactly operating from wheelchairs, were much older and from an entirely different tradition than their professional heirs in the Gulf. Smith, in his Para beret, looks like a boyish major rather than a major general. Both Cordingley and Hammerbeck are likewise quite youthful and energetic leaders in their forties rather than the doddering and fussy old brigadiers of the past.

1 (British) Armoured Division Order of Battle

4 Armoured Brigade
14/20 King's Royal Hussars
1 Royal Scots
3 Royal Regiment of Fusiliers
2 Field Regiment RA

7 Armoured Brigade
Royal Scots Dragoon Guards

A Ferret patrols out west, a USMC CH-53 in the background. The little scout car is quite capable of reaching 50mph without difficulty, on or off road, and has excellent fuel economy which makes it a natural for such kinds of guard duty. Bob Morrison: Military Scene

Brigadier Christopher Hammerbeck, commander of 4 Armoured Brigade, and his trusty Land-Rover. The brigadier has served as a tanker for most of his long career. Bob Morrison: Military Scene

Queen's Royal Irish Hussars
1 Staffordshire Regiment
40 Field Regiment RA

Divisional Troops
16/5 Queen's Royal Lancers
26 Field Regiment, Royal Artillery (RA)
32 Heavy Regiment RA
39 Heavy Regiment RA
The Life Guards
9/12 Royal Lancers
17/21 Lancers
4 Royal Tank Regiment
1 Grenadier Guards
1 Scots Guards
1 Devonshire & Dorset Regiment
1 Prince of Wales' Own Regiment of Yorkshire
1 Queen's Own Royal Highlanders
1 Royal Green Jackets

One after another, people and units received their orders, assembled their kit, wrote their letters, said their good-byes, and waited for their aircraft. They all waited through the searing autumn for the Iraqi invasion that should have come, but didn't. They trained, maintained the tanks and guns, plotted, and schemed. The rumors circulated and units trained for missions that would never be executed. Everybody waited through false alarms and little crises.

On 17 January the air war began, and 1 Division waited some more—for a counterattack with Iraq's massed armor, or with chemical or biological weapons, or even a nuclear device.

After months of training alongside the US Marines, and waiting to attack alongside the most British-like of American forces, 1 Division was assigned to fight the ground war with VII Corps to the west. On 14 February, 1 Division joined the massive, secret road march far to the west, to a desolate piece of real estate called Area KEYES. Here some of the waiting ended and some began; operational orders were issued, sand-table exercises conducted, final ammunition uploads were delivered, and last letters home were written.

To the left and right of the Brits, across the whole southern border of Iraq and Kuwait, in battle array, were 600,000 soldiers from over forty nations—more than forty divisions of armor, artillery, infantry, engineers, combat aviation, transport, medical, and other units. To the left of 1 Division, on line, was the American 1st Infantry Division (Mechanized); on the right, the American 1st Cavalry Division.

To the front lay a series of minefields, artillery positions, bunker complexes, and unknown quantities of enemy troops with unknown quantities of conventional and perhaps chemical weapons. To the front were enemy commanders with unknown intentions and abilities. To the front, on that cold, damp morning lay victory or defeat, life or death, success or failure—for one side or the other, as yet undecided.

Mission

The mission for these new Desert Rats was one essential role in a play with a cast of thousands. While the American XVIII Corps attacks in its huge left hook from the west and the US Marines and Arab Coalition forces push up through the most difficult, heavily defended parts of Kuwait, 1 Division and the VII Corps are assigned to go up the middle.

GOC Rupert Smith, division commander, issues his plan to the subordinate commands:

The DEPTH BATTLE will be fought about 50km out, using attack helicopters and medium reconnaissance regiments.

The CONTACT BATTLE will be fought by the two armored brigades, 4 and 7—each brigade to be committed sequentially. While one is in action, the other will be refurbishing with fuel, ammunition, food.

Objectives will be assigned that are suitable for a single brigade to secure with no more than ten percent British losses on each objective. This will insure sufficient force conservation for the accomplishment of the entire mission for 1 Armoured Division.

This is a major break from plans and procedure in Germany and, for the senior commanders, is a new way of conducting business. It has required additional training, as well as new procedures and staff coordination. The key commanders and staff have spent endless hours at sand-table exercises and conferences trying to sort out how to make it all happen. Then, at the

UK 1 Armoured Division commander Major-General Rupert Smith—a boyish-looking 47 years old during the operation. General Smith, in the grand British tradition, is something of an odd duck—a member of the Parachute regiment (the legendary Paras) with extensive training and experience in armor. An expert in Soviet tank tactics, he adapted Warsaw Pact doctrine to British purposes in the Gulf. He holds the Queen's Gallantry Medal for the rescue of another officer after the explosion of a car bomb in 1978. Military Scene

Lieutenant General Sir Peter de la Billiere, overall commander of the British forces assembled to evict the Iraqis from Kuwait. Military Scene

On the way! A Multiple Launch Rocket System cuts loose a round down range. The MLRS provides extremely mobile, automated, long-range, and effective area fire. This rocket has a range of over nineteen miles and contains 644 submunitions, each of which is capable of killing a tank. British Army

end of January, the British mission had finally come down from on high:

> MISSION: 1 (British) Armoured Division will attack through the 1st (US) Infantry Division (Mechanized) to defeat the enemy tactical reserves in order to protect the right flank of the US VII Corps.

This mission requires close coordination with US forces. The US 1st Infantry Division is asked to provide eight cleared lanes for British forces through the minefields. It also provokes several extremely complicated passage-of-lines exercises, two at night, that result in what the soldiers called "the mother of all traffic jams."

The final mission is received by the brigade commanders on 24 February, the day before the 1 (British) Armoured Division will go into battle. After five months of waiting and training his force, Brigadier Cordingley discovers that he has exactly twenty-five minutes to produce an attack plan for his first objective. "At this point, I didn't even know which brigade would go through first, although I did know that we would go north and 4 Brigade would cross the southern part of the route."

This mission is scheduled to kick off on G + 1, a day after the ground war begins. 1 Div will follow the US 1st Mechanized Infantry through the breech after the American combat engineers clear the minefields and fire trenches. For most of the Coalition forces, the order to move out comes out during the wee hours of the twenty-fourth, but not for the British forces.

At 1000 hours on G-day, while the curtain goes up across the whole front, the Desert Rats are still waiting for their debut. General Rupert Smith convenes his orders group at his headquarters in Assembly Area RAY, one last chance for the senior commanders and their staffs to ask questions, express doubts, verify instructions. The commanders return to their units, and the waiting continues.

But the attack is going faster than expected and the US 1st Mech's breaching operation is completed far ahead of schedule. The order comes down: Prepare to move up to the staging area at 1400 hours, fifteen hours ahead of schedule. The forty-kilometer shift with the help of tank transporters had been planned for the next day but, in the grand tradition of war, the very first part of the plan is discarded before the enemy is even met. The brigades, which had scheduled briefings and orders-group meetings, suddenly discover that they will have to postpone these essential discussions until they are safely installed in Assembly Area RAY.

The units move out on their own tracks, execute a hectic passage of lines with their left-flank neighbor, and roll across the soggy desert toward the sound of guns. While the tanks race forward to meet the new schedule, the logistics units that make up the tail of the beast, scurrying frantically to keep up. But at least part of the waiting is over.

The teeth of the beast are three battle groups, all task-organized from brigade assets. Only the Queen's Royal Irish Hussars remain a pure unit—tanks only. The Staffords, normally a mechanized infantry battalion, have successfully pilfered two tank squadrons to keep the lads in the Warriors company, one each from the Scots Dragoon Guards and the other from the Queen's Royal Irish Hussars.

The Rats, feeling ratty in the cold, with rain and wind pelting everything, wait while the war proceeds without them. Brigadier Cordingley tries to sleep, without success. At 2200 hours he attempts to relax with a game of chess with his tank operator, Capt. Richard Kemp, and the brigadier wins. "His mind must have been on other things," Cordingley says, "as it is *quite* difficult to lose against me."

Outside artillery batteries are firing prep missions, the noise of the big 155mm guns adding to the racket from the rain and wind. Those able to, sleep fitfully.

At 0630, 7 Armoured Brigade commanders assemble for an orders-group discussion of attack plans, with Cordingley presiding and the battle group and regimental commanders attending. Lieutenant Colonel Arthur Denaro commands the Queen's Royal Irish Hussars (tanks), Lieutenant Colonel John Sharples the Royal Scots Dragoon Guards (tanks also), and Lieutenant Colonel Charles Rogers the Staffords (mechanized infantry); Lieutenant Colonel Rory Clayton commands 40 Field Artillery Regiment, the guns. Everyone is dressed in NBC kit as a precaution against the feared use of chemical agents. Later in the day the brigade will assault an objective about which very little is actually known—a communications site that probably holds a headquarters site, a logistics unit, and elements of an enemy brigade.

G + 1 1515—Line of Departure

The 7 Armoured Brigade attempts to get through the breech at 0800 but is held up by the throng. It makes the attempt again about noon. The lead units finally drive into their forming-up position in front of the line of departure, PL NEW JERSEY, at 1430.

At 1515 on the second day of the war, Brigadier Patrick Cordingley's 7 Brigade is ordered to advance across the LD (line of departure) with the Queen's Royal Irish Hussars in the lead. It will take hours for the brigade to get through. Cordingley's brigade surges out of the bridgehead, the Queen's Royal Irish Hussars covering the first fifteen miles in an hour with two helicopters assisting in route reconnaissance, as much to unplug the bottleneck as anything.

Number 4 Brigade will wait until evening, about 1715 hours, to follow. At last 1 Div is off to war, and Cordingley can report via encrypted radio "Lima Delta," that the line of departure has been crossed. The armored vehicles roar through the lanes cleared by the American engineers, between the white tapes marking safe routes through the mine fields. When safely

Brigadier P. A. J. Cordingley, 7 Armoured Brigade commander, attends to the barrage of paperwork that is the curse of command. P. A. J. Cordingley

The first Challenger tank from the Queen's Royal Irish Hussars rolls onto the ship that will carry it from *Germany to the Gulf and off to war.* Bob Morrison: Military Scene

across, 7 Brigade pauses to refuel from the combat support fuel tankers of the battle group. The Challengers of the Scots Dragoon Guards and Queen's Royal Irish Hussars battle groups pause while the Staffords are stuck in a traffic jam far to the rear.

For 7 Brigade the first objective will be COPPER NORTH, about 30 kilometers ahead. En route, the brigade trades shots with scattered small units of infantry and isolated armor before reaching their pre-attack assembly area. First contact came at about 1800, made by two of the infantry company's attached to the Scots Dragoon Guards battle group, A and D Companies of the 1 Staffordshire Regiment. According to the intelligence summary, COPPER NORTH was alleged to be a fairly simple problem, not much more than a communications site, but as the Warriors assaulted it, COPPER NORTH became a *complicated* complex.

Second Lieutenant Richard Telfer, MC

The weak, gloomy daylight faded early on the evening of G+1, and for the Scots Dragoon Guards the waiting was decidedly over. As the Challengers and Warriors closed with the communications complex in the middle of the objective, all normal visibility disappeared in pouring rain and an inky blackness that precluded any kind of normal navigation. But the tanks TOGS thermal sights provided enough information for the attack. And through the TOGS sights the tank commanders and gunners began to identify enemy troops and armor on the objective. What they saw were long berms and trenches; even without the TOGS you could easily see the tracers from the enemy machine gun fire coming at the Scots Dragoon Guards and Staffords. The battle-group commander, Lieutenant Colonel John Sharples, received reports of intense enemy activity on the objective, with many soldiers running around between vehicles. When the Challengers and Warriors fired, the fire was promptly returned.

One of first on the objective was a young, extremely junior second lieutenant named Richard Telfer, commanding the lead troop of Challengers. Through his TOGS, Telfer could see large numbers of enemy soldiers and vehicles roaring around like a nest of agitated ants; he reported the contact to his battle-group commander, Lieutenant Colonel Sharples. "A" Company of the Staffords and Telfer's troop of Scots Dragoon Guards were ordered to assault the position immediately, with Telfer in the lead. While one of the three Challengers chose this moment to have a breakdown, and the other is securing a flank, Telfer drives up onto the

Brigadier Cordingley conspires with USMC General Walt Boomer during the build-up phase of the operation—Operation Granby for British forces, Desert Shield for the American participants. A strong mutual affection developed between American Marines and British Army personnel during the months of the build up based on the high levels of professionalism in both communities. It was a disappointment for both when the Brits were given a change of mission that prevented them from attacking into Kuwait alongside the Marines, as originally planned. USMC

British tanks, freshly painted, wait to be driven onto the ships that will take them to desert war. The Iraqi invasion of Kuwait and subsequent United Nations resolution provoked British forces in Germany to a frenzy of preparation for battle. Bob Morrison: Military Scene

position, leading the Staffords Warrior-borne infantry into the complex, destroying the Iraqi tanks and APCs first, then debussing the infantry to clean out the bunkers and trenches.

For the infantry it was like stepping out into a void. Bullets fly everywhere. Only when the enemy vehicles start catching fire does anyone have any illumination. Even so, the soldiers clear the bunkers methodically. For the next

British Navy electronic-warfare unit set up in the desert. Units like this were used in an electronic-deception campaign to convince the enemy units that 1 Division was still near the Gulf coast by recording and retransmitting normal radio traffic after the move to the west was done. Bob Morrison: Military Scene

forty-five minutes, the task force fires up the objective. Telfer's Challenger was the center of the bulls'-eye for the enemy and small arms fire pinged off the hull of the tank. By the light of burning enemy vehicles the Staffords swept across the position, directed by Telfer, observing through the thermal sight and firing on targets of opportunity.

Major Knapper's infantry worked across the objective with rifles, fragmentation, and WP (white phosphorus) incendiary grenades and the CLAW close assault weapon. After all the training, waiting and worrying, the doubts and fears, the Staffords finally discovered what war really would be like, and it turned out to be frightening, exhilarating, damn hard work. They cleared trenches first with the CLAW, then L2 frag grenades, finally WP and automatic rifle fire.

During the course of the action one of the infantry privates, Mark Eason, was surprised by an enemy soldier who popped up from a trench and fired. Eason felt a great whacking blow to the chest and was knocked violently to the ground where he lay for a few moments, thinking dire thoughts, waiting for dear life to ebb away. Rather to Private Eason's surprise, his respiration continued and a thorough exploration of his person discovered no leaks or breaks, although the soreness amidships was real enough. A little further exploration discovered a hole in a spare magazine for his SA80 rifle; it had stopped the bullet that could have killed him. And with that, Private Eason hopped up and went back to war.

An Iraqi tank company bravely counterattacked. All its tanks were promptly destroyed by the Scots Dragoon Guards. The objective was finally cleared by 2200 hours. Three other Staffords were not as lucky as Private Eason and were wounded in the action. Two Military Crosses would be awarded for actions on the objective—one to the infantry company commander, Maj. Simon Knapper, the other to Second Lieutenant Telfer.

The battle group's next objective lay in the distance, a large tent complex around a water hole that was suspected of being a field hospital—although no one was sure. A halt was called until first light.

On to Zinc

The other two battle groups comprising 7 Brigade, 1 Staffordshire Regiment and Queen's Royal Irish Hussars drove around the COPPER NORTH objective while the Scots Dragoon Guards went about their business in the dark. ZINC was thought to contain a whole enemy brigade. If so, it should be a tough nut for Cordingley's depleted force, what with the Scots Dragoon Guards battle group momentarily occupied with its first combat.

It is a troublesome moment, this lack of reliable information about ZINC, but Cordingley has at least one major comfort: the entire artillery assets of 1 Div—five regiments of British artillery, plus, if necessary, an entire American artillery brigade—which works out

to more weight of fire than Field Marshal Montgomery had at the battle of El Alamein for his entire army, all on-call for a single brigade.

In the middle of the night, Cordingley and his artillery commander, the commander of 40 Field Regiment, make plans to use this resource, then follow up the barrage immediately with an assault on ZINC, a rapid, sweeping attack that comes in from east to west, cleaning up anything left on the position. It is a kind of command problem quite different than practiced in NATO exercises, one well suited for the British system where the commander decides and the staff makes it go; as Brigadier Cordingley explains:

"You didn't have to be Rommel to come up with a plan like that—it was perfectly logical. And it could be made very quickly . . . the staff had nothing to do with the making of that plan, but what they had to do then was to put in the control measures to make it possible. The report

Troops from a variety of 4 Brigade units model some of the berets and kit popular in the Gulf. British soldiers don't really wear a uniform in the conventional sense; individuals are permitted a lot of latitude in their *battle dress, much of which is often purchased from private vendors by the soldier.* Bob Morrison: Military Scene

lines, lines of exploitation, the boundaries between battle groups—the sort of things I didn't want to get involved in."

Cordingley brought up tanks from Queen's Royal Irish Hussars and prodded them up toward the objective for a peek. What they saw was a bit disconcerting: a major defensive position. At about 0015 hours on G + 2 the huge M110 eight-inch howitzers, the M109 155mm SP guns, and Multiple Launch Rocket System fire a prep mission on the objective, saturating it with huge high-explosive projectiles and thousands of the deadly submunitions. It was the first shots in anger for both the old eight-inch gun, in British

service for three decades, and the new rocket system, in the British arsenal for only six months. The enemy positions are blanketed with fire, the nearest impacts only a kilometer or so from Cordingley and his tanks.

Under the devastating cover of their heavy weight of fire, the Staffords and Queen's Royal Irish Hussars move up on the objective, then, as the barrage lifts, rapidly assault the position with minimal objections from the current tenants. By 0530 on G + 2 the brigade (minus) had cleared ZINC and by 0800 was at PL LAVENDER, facing east and ready to move. The fight on ZINC resulted in the capture of thirty tanks, the

A Ferret scout car at a forward maintenance shop area, waiting for the call to action. The Ferret ought to be a candidate for an antique car collectors' club—it is *a design that is about fifty years old—but remains a fast, sturdy, well-liked vehicle that was at home on the desert.* Bob Morrison: Military Scene

destruction of sixteen APCs, and 1,850 prisoners of war in the bag. The confidence level of the Rats was rapidly rising.

4 Brigade, G + 1

While Brigadier Cordingley and his band of merry men are charging across the northern part of the 1 Div zone, poor 4 Brigade, Brigadier Christopher Hammerbeck officiating, still have a bit of waiting to do. At last, at 1930 hours on a cold, wet, extremely dark night of G + 1, their lead elements finally cross the line of departure with 14/20 King's Royal Hussars (Colonel Michael Vickery commanding) crossing the obstacle belt at Axis Hawk and 1 Battalion The Royal Scots Dragoon Guards (Lieutenant Colonel Iain Johnstone commanding) going across at Axis Tartan further south. And it's about damn time, too—the war is now two days old, no chemical weapons or other disasters have been revealed, and it is time to get on with it.

The poor 4 Brigade has yet one other problem before getting up steam. Straight out of the box, a huge convoy of ammunition trucks comes blundering along across the brigades' route-of-march just across the line of departure. The encounter separates some of the leaders from the followers and delays the program for yet another hour. Number 4 Brigade is just about ready to engage the next thing that gets in their way, friendly or otherwise.

Brigadier Hammerbeck's mission originally is to engage units on an objective just beyond the line of departure called BRONZE, but that is modified just before the show starts, to clear it— a much tougher problem, one that will take extra time. On the way, however, the brigade discovers some pesky Iraqis who need to be dealt with first; 14/20 King's Royal Hussars destroy an enemy communications site and artillery position while 1 Royal Scots arrive uninvited at another local artillery position and depart after wrecking the place.

B Squadron, 14/20 Hussars, discovers that HESH rounds work well against machine-gun emplacements, and that the fin-stabilized 120mm main gun round will go straight through a T-55 turret and out the other side. They also

A 7 Brigade sentry with a GPMG endures another tour of incredible boredom. Bob Morrison: Military Scene

discover how nice it is to outrange the enemy tankers, whose guns and gunsights are not equal to the British version. They discover that some of the enemy tanks have fired five or more rounds at the Rats without scoring before they are hit by the first Challenger round.

Major Andrew Gillespie, O Battery Commander, takes a heavy machine gun hit to his Warrior turret, producing a loud bang inside but without damaging anything more than the crew's composure.

By 0230 on G + 2, 4 Brigade has finally gotten to show its stuff and Objective BRONZE is clear; the battle groups have destroyed twelve tanks, eleven guns, and twenty light armor and thin-skin vehicles.

The 4 Brigade moves on to the southern part of Objective Copper, COPPER SOUTH. It is only supposed to have an artillery battery to clear, an enemy force not likely to exceed a single company. About midnight on G + 2 the lead elements of the battle groups make initial contact with the enemy forces and discover that, instead of the few guns and troops expected, there is a whole tank battle group to deal with, including at least twenty-five main battle tanks, plus armored personnel carriers, artillery, logistics-support vehicles, and many troops, all visible only through the thermal sight systems.

The Challengers opened fire on the tanks first, with awesome effect. One after another, the enemy armor came unglued. The 14/20 King's Royal Hussars attacked across the objective, firing on the move. It is a pursuit battle, a running gunfight that lasts till what should be first light. By 0530 on the dank, dark morning of G + 2 COPPER SOUTH is clear of resistance, POWs (including two enemy division com-

manders) are moving to the rear and 4 Brigade moves off again toward the east.

SitRep: G + 2 0800

The situation for the two British brigades and 1 Division at 0800 on G + 2 finds 7 Armoured Brigade finished with ZINC and poised to attack Objectives PLATINUM and LEAD later in the day. The 4 Brigade has regrouped and is ready to attack BRASS, STEEL, and TUNGSTEN.

4 Brigade, G + 2: Brass, Steel, and Tungsten

The next impediment to the 4 Brigade's eastward migration was a nasty bit of territory identified as Objective BRASS, alleged to be the

Brigadier Hammerbeck's 4 Brigade command Warrior AFV at rest in the desert. Its clean, fresh appearance, with camouflage nets neatly stowed and everything all neat and tidy, would soon become grimy and *a bit disorderly—just like the crew—after the dash toward Kuwait City began.* Bob Morrison: Military Scene

home of the entire enemy 52nd Armored Brigade. The western portion of BRASS holds an infantry and armor battle group with approximately twelve tanks and additional APCs, Soviet-supplied MTLBs, all effectively hidden in deep holes and fighting positions. The center holds a tank-heavy unit with about thirty tanks, plus MTLBs and artillery. Farther to the eastern portion of the enemy complex is yet more artillery.

The attack will be executed in phases, one battle group after another. It begins, however, with a massive artillery barrage from 26 Field Artillery Regiment to suppress resistance on the position with drenching fire while 4 Armoured Brigade's battle groups assault. Not until the lead elements are actually on the objective is the artillery fire lifted with the infantry debussing within range of the enemy positions. The combined shock effect of the artillery barrage and the arrival of a bunch of raving Scotsmen on the doorstep is all that is required for most of the enemy soldiers to surrender.

Number 1 Royal Scots begins the show with the Warriors moving first due north, then turning hard toward the southeast to come in behind the enemy positions. They quickly spot six obsolete but highly dangerous T-55 tanks through the murk and open fire, destroying them all. Then the infantry was debussed from the Warriors to clear the trench lines. Twenty-five MTLBs are caught in their holes and destroyed by B Company until the company commander, Major John Potter, gets a report of enemy tanks in the area. Potter's lads are quickly reinforced with a troop of Challengers, and the whole assembly goes dashing through the enemy position, firing like crazy—machine guns against the trenches and bunkers, the cannon fire from the 30mm Rarden guns against the Soviet-built light armor.

"Brassing Up"

Enemy soldiers tried to engage with automatic weapons and rocket-propelled grenades but without the intended effect. The Warrior's armor deflected the small arms fire and rocket-

A Centurion AVRE 165 tank recovery vehicle passes burned-out Iraqi armor. The large quantities of flammables aboard armored vehicles (fuel, ammunition, *hydraulic fluid, rubber, and—sadly—human bodies, which burn rather well) all contribute to a very messy battlefield.* Military Scene

The Staffordshire Regiment maintained the traditional observation of its regimental day on the desert on 21 December 1990. British Army

propelled grenades while the night-vision devices used by the gunners and commanders observed every muzzle flash, every gun position. Instead of beating off the assault, these gunners called attention to themselves and were promptly "brassed up" by the Warrior's 7.62mm Hughes chain gun; if that didn't achieve the desired effect, the 30mm Rarden cannon with three-round clips of HE did. One hardcore Iraqi continued to fire after the chain-gun treatment, so all fourteen Warriors from B Company launched 30mm HE, bringing a new meaning to the expression "overkill," but achieving the desired results.

The commander of 1 Royal Scots, Lieutenant Colonel Iain Johnstone, watches the T-55s brew up while listening to the pitter-pat of enemy small arms fire bouncing off the slender armor of his Warrior. The light from the burning vehicles, along with the illumination rounds fired by artillery, reveal hundreds of enemy soldiers surrendering.

Major Gillespie's Warrior takes two near misses from an Iraqi T-55 that materializes only 400 meters away. One round goes past the turret, over the rear deck, the next round over the front. Gillespie's gunner fires at the tank with the 30mm cannon without visible effect until the battle-group commander intervenes with a 120mm round from his Challenger. The T-55 promptly blows up.

Elsewhere, an MTLB has been artfully installed by the enemy and can't be destroyed except the old-fashioned way, by infantry—in this case, B Company's 5 Platoon. The platoon sergeant, Thomas Gorrian, and Private Tam Gow crawl up to the rear of the emplacement. While their mates are firing up the immediate vicinity with their SA80s, Gow fires a CLAW into the back doors of the vehicle from fifteen meters away. There is a tremendous crash and flash from the weapon which largely destroys the enemy APC; Gow doesn't actually *see* the impact, though, because he ducks just before firing. But he sits up again and tosses in a WP grenade. The MTLB is now quite beyond repair. The platoon goes off to clear two other bunkers, then it is back on the bus. Gow will receive the Military Medal for the exploit.

While 1 Royal Scots is busy with all this, the lads from 14/20 King's Royal Hussars are swinging around from the north, back westward to take out the bulk of the enemy forces through the back door. It involves a march, out in the open and in what passes for daylight, across ten kilometers of desert against an immense enemy position spread across thirty square kilometers, a position known on the battle maps as BRASS 3. They take out another twenty-five tanks and twenty APCs. BRASS 1 is subdued by 1200, BRASS 2 by about 1300, courtesy of 14/20 King's Royal Hussars; and by 1500 the eastern part of the complex, BRASS 3, is also taken, this one by 3 Battalion, The Royal Regiment of Fusiliers who then drive on toward Objective STEEL, which they take without assistance but with devastating losses.

At around 1500 hours on G + 2 an American A-10 Thunderbolt II close-air-support aircraft mistakes 3 Royal Regiment of Fusiliers armor for enemy and attacks, rolling in on the targets from only 1,500 feet to deliver Maverick missiles. Nine British soldiers are killed, seven are wounded, and two Warrior APCs are destroyed by sharp, sudden explosions that the regimental commander suspects were the result of anti-tank mines. Some of the dead include soldiers attempting rescues. It is the biggest loss of British soldiers during the war, and the most avoidable. But an hour later the objective is cleared and the advance continues.

Tungsten

Tired, dirty, exhilarated, apprehensive, the Rats continue their assault, acquiring a kind of momentum of pursuit; the Rats are beginning to wish the Iraqis will just surrender or else stand, fight, and die. Instead, the enemy mostly runs, fights delaying actions, or surrenders—occasionally doing all three at once, to the consternation of all concerned.

After less than a full day of combat, the 4 Brigade has covered about seventy-two miles, destroyed an enemy brigade, and collected about 4,000 POWs including two division commanders.

Late on the evening of G + 2, the 4 Brigade moves up to its line of departure for the attack on TUNGSTEN. Before the festivities can begin, an above-ground oil pipeline has to be negotiated with the assistance of the engineers. Then the heavy artillery of the division, augmented by the US Army National Guard's MLRS and eight-inch guns from 142 Artillery Brigade fires a prep mission on the objective. Batteries from 39 Heavy Regiment, Royal Artillery, 26 Field Artillery Regiment, and 2 Field Regiment participate. For nearly an hour they pour fire on the objective. Enemy artillery ammunition explodes beside the guns. The ground is carpeted with flashes, smoke, dust, sparks, and flame. The sound of individual guns blend into a continuous roar. Although the Rats don't know it yet, 90 percent of the enemy gunners are killed or wounded by the barrage, plus seventy guns are taken out, effectively neutralizing the artillery unit and much of the rest of the enemy force on the objective.

Then the assault is launched. Once more, 1 Royal Scots and 3 Royal Fusiliers drive off, destroying any active armor or resisting infan-

try. Finally, to encourage any doubters still hiding out, the assault elements fire three big 155mm artillery rounds into the complex, then broadcast a call for surrender in Arabic. It was a form of therapy that needed several applications, but ultimately proved to be successful. Objective TUNGSTEN was declared secure at 0430 on the morning of the twenty-seventh, G + 3.

Lieutenant Richard Telfer, MC (Military Cross), commanded A Troop, Scots Dragoon Guards, a component of 4 Brigade. The lieutenant won his Military Cross by leading an attack on a large enemy complex early in the ground war although the other two tanks supporting him were out of action. With enemy small arms fire bouncing off his tank, the lieutenant led and directed a successful assault against a large enemy force on an objective called COPPER.

7 Brigade, G + 2: Platinum and Lead

The plan for Brigadier Cordingley's brigade, with its three battle groups, on the third day of the ground war was a complicated one. PLATINUM is a huge complex, full of enemy assets. It is divided into two sections, west (PLATINUM 1) and east (PLATINUM 2). A battlefield-prep bombing mission executed by the US Air Force is scheduled to precede a phased attack by 7 Brigade's three battle groups. First, the Queen's Royal Irish Hussars will assault the western portion, followed by Scots Dragoon Guards attacking PLATINUM 2. The first phase kicks off about noon.

The attack seems to completely surprise the enemy on the position who scurry about frantically, shooting ineffectively—except to further annoy the visiting Rats. There seems to be a combination of panic, counterattack, and confusion operating in the enemy unit. The recon platoon owns and operates the MILAN anti-tank missiles and starts engaging the enemy armor on the position. One missile strikes the rear of a T-55 tank, lifting the rear of the vehicle off the ground and blasting the tank commander out the hatch, forty feet into the air. The other four MILANs open up, wreaking havoc on the MTLBs and other Iraqi armored personnel carriers.

An engineer detachment shows up and starts destroying enemy tanks by using cutting torches to slice off gun barrels and break tracks.

"Bombing up" a Challenger. Resupply and rearming was provided by logistics support units following closely behind the lead elements. According to its crews, the Challenger is a much better tank than its American cousin, the M1 Abrams. Both did well enough, although one Challenger gunner probably takes the prize for long-range tank killing—a verified 5,100-meter shot that scored a bulls-eye on the first try. British Army

While they are busy with this chore, a couple of enemy T-55s materialize out of the gloom and—offended by this abuse of their armor—start to chase the engineers around the position until they are distracted by more important things.

Now the major tactical problem quickly turns into dealing with the hordes of POWs. Those who aren't killed or captured try to escape to the east—a tactical error, since the second phase of the mission now begins.

At about 1300 hours, the Staffords launch their attack on PLATINUM 2, sweeping down from the north and sweeping the enemy from their positions while the Queen's Royal Irish Hussars provide artillery fire support. By 1430, the objective is completely secure with 1,500 prisoners in the bag. The Staffords press on toward their next objective, LEAD, with the other two battle groups, Queen's Royal Irish Hussars and Scots Dragoon Guards, moving up on the left.

Late in the afternoon, while reports of mass surrenders are coming over the battle-group communications nets, the Staffords bump hard into a company of enemy who aren't ready to quit without a fight. Unfortunately, they are mixed in with a bunch who are trying to quit. Some troops from C Company, 1 Staffords, de-buss to accept the surrender of one lot of these while a few die-hards choose the moment to open up on the Brits. Private Carl Moult, an eighteen-year-old from Burton-on-Trent, is killed on LEAD, struck and instantly killed by an RPG-7 rocket-propelled grenade. The round strikes its original target, a Warrior, which catches fire with the driver and some of the troops still aboard. One of the bystanders, Darrin Chant, a Grenadier Guardsman temporarily attached to the unit, rescues the Warrior's crew and tries to put out the fire.

In other wars, and with other armies, such an event would result in the wholesale slaughter of the entire enemy presence in the area as revenge for Private Moult's death. Instead, the enemy fire is identified, isolated, and suppressed while the surrender of the enemy is accepted. In the bag are old men on crutches and a bawling thirteen-year-old boy, plus two fat

Although it never materialized, the threat of chemical and biological warfare was real and serious. Had the Iraqis actually used their stocks of chemical and biological weapons, hundreds of thousands of coalition casualties might have been suffered. These troops are getting accustomed to their NBC suits. British Army

enemy colonels. Over a thousand POWs are processed and sent to the rear. Moult's body is recovered, placed in one of the vehicles, and after four hours of fighting, his mates finish clearing the place by 1740 hours and press on to the next phase line, SMASH, ready for the next mission.

SitRep, 0800 hours, G + 3

The morning of the twenty-seventh finds both brigades facing east across the Wadi al Batin, grimy and sore and profoundly, utterly sleepy. Just after midnight, 7 Armoured Brigade moves out across Phase Line SMASH for an attack on the next objective, VARSITY.

The troops in the Warriors are able to nap as the vehicles wallow across the desert—there isn't much else to do. But the tank crewmen and particularly the commanders, and the people who support the commanders with information, are all in zombie-mode from the hours of alert-

The British Army brought its traditions along to the Gulf, just as it has for centuries. This piper is from 4 Brigade. British Army

ness. People are getting irritable and are beginning to make mistakes. It is a dangerous time, and one full of opportunities—historically, the time where victors suddenly are vanquished, where defeat is snatched from the jaws of success. The pursuit continues. Ahead, according to the intelligence officers, are the enemy's first string defensive line, the Republican Guards. For the leaders and the followers alike there is still the gnawing doubt that perhaps the real war has not yet begun.

But to counteract those doubts is a growing confidence in the whole combination of people, weapons, and plan. Losses have been far less than anyone imagined possible. Young soldiers who doubted their own ability to endure fire and to kill discovered that they could, after all, do what they had trained to do. When circumstances required, heroes appeared where needed, from the ranks of the officers and the enlisted soldiers both. Despite appalling

A 4 Brigade Air Defence Regiment Spartan. Bob Morrison: Military Scene

124

weather conditions, the Rats discovered that they could see much better than their enemy and could engage him effectively while he was essentially blind.

Weapons never previously used in combat, like the Challenger's main gun, proved to be almost magical in their effectiveness, with 3,000-meter kills becoming fairly routine. One gunner from the Royal Scots Dragoon Guards, as a kind of test, fired on an enemy tank at 5,100 meters—approximately twice the normal range—and killed it with the first round. A captured Iraqi artillery brigade commander reported that the air campaign had destroyed thirteen of his 100 guns, but the Rats heavy guns and MLRS had destroyed another seventy. And the marvelous GPS sets, despite occasional breakdowns, provided a kind of navigational precision previously impossible, which allowed for faster movement and more precise targeting.

For the senior commanders in 1 Division and for the whole campaign, the war began to get interesting, a classic pursuit battle with a routed enemy. But for the battle groups in 4 and 7 Armoured Brigades, from the squaddies to the commanders, the battle was to stay awake, to prepare for the next objective, to be ready for surprises—and to drive on toward the east.

People are tired everywhere. Number 4 Armoured Brigade gets *extremely* contradictory orders from VII Corps, putting the staff in a dither. In the Wadi there is another example of the fog of war: the thermal sights pick up vehicles approaching where no friendly vehicles are supposed to be. Number 14/20 Hussars opens fire at long range, then seconds later the

The ammunition for one Warrior (B Company, 1 Battalion, The Staffordshire Regiment) is laid out for *inspection and inventory before the ground campaign kicks off.* British Army

order to check fire comes over the net; the "enemy" are logistic support vehicles, doing what they've been ordered to do, but somebody has failed to inform the tanks. Two Spartan command and control vehicles have been set afire but no one hurt. The 4 Armoured Brigade is ordered to take a break in place while VII Corps figures out what the next mission should be.

Number 7 Armoured Brigade attacks VARSITY at 0630, routing the enemy while, to the south, 4 Armoured Brigade gets to regroup and refuel its people and vehicles. Then at 1400, 4 Armoured Brigade is ordered to attack the enemy forces pushed out of VARSITY by the earlier attack. There is not much to attack. Number 4 Armoured Brigade is ordered to stand fast on VARSITY at 1600.

Just before midnight, at 2330 on G + 3, an order comes over the radio from 1 Division commander Rupert Smith with a new mission for the brigades: attack east to Objective CO-BALT, astride the Kuwait City—Basra Road, to cut routes from Kuwait City to prevent the Iraqi Army from escape north. At 0400 hours, the mission is assigned to 7 Armoured Brigade, supported by MLRS and combat support sufficient for independent operations; they will move at first light.

While Cordingley and company are getting ready to travel again, the radio nets add some additional information to spur the proceedings: a cease-fire is scheduled for 0800 . . . not much time to block the road north, if it was to be done at all.

The brigade hits the road again, with visions of winning the Great International Desert Rally & Grand Prix of 1991. Let 4 Armoured Brigade sleep; we're off to Kuwait City!

Cordingley leads with a squadron of Queen's Dragoon Guards and the three battle groups up abreast for speed and flank security. The lead squadron along with elements of the Queen's Royal Irish Hussars roll onto COBALT about half an hour before the cease-fire after a dash of forty-five kilometers. As offensive operations cease, the Rats get a good look at the effect of the invasion and its aftermath. There are destroyed vehicles everywhere, dead enemy soldiers here

RAF Puma helicopters provided medium-lift support throughout the campaign. Bob Morrison: Military Scene

The fates and fortunes of war, north of Kuwait City. Iraqi armor burned and rusting on the road to Basra.

When military units panic odd things happen. This enemy tank was driven up on a traffic barrier during the rout of Iraqi forces out of Kuwait toward Basra and Iraq to the north.

and there. Black smoke from the burning oil wells provide a suitably theatrical atmosphere. There is a noticeable lack of glee from the victors.

Rupert Smith arrives around noon with the 1 Div headquarters element. Number 7 Brigade displaces once again, to the south and Objective SODIUM, to tidy up its control of the road and to tie in with the US Marines just across the tactical boundary in Kuwait City.

Number 7 Armoured Brigade's sappers start the nasty job of cleaning up the mess in the Mutla Pass where hundreds of vehicles, mostly stolen and loaded with looted goods, litter the road. Many of the looters litter the road, too, and the whole hellish mess must be tidied up.

SitRep, 0800 Hours, G + 4

The cease-fire finds the escape route north from Kuwait City solidly blocked by 7 Armoured Brigade astride the road and 4 Armoured Brigade just twenty miles to the west at Phase Line SWORD.

Brigadier Cordingley has brought his brigade across 180 miles (300 kilometers) of desert battlefield in sixty-eight hours, fought six major engagements or battle-group actions at a cost of two dead and fifteen wounded. Number 7 Armoured Brigade destroyed more than ninety enemy tanks plus large numbers of light armor and thin-skinned vehicles, and took over 3,000 POWs. As the brigadier later observes, "Of my 117 tanks, 104 were fit, as were all the Warriors. We could easily have gone on to Basra."

Brigadier Hammerbeck had taken 4 Armoured Brigade nearly one hundred kilometers across some nasty ground in the last day, despite conflicting orders and fatigue. They had come 350 kilometers in ninety-seven hours, averaging three kilometers an hour in a combat environment. Number 4 Brigade had destroyed three enemy divisions in the process, including the dismantling of huge numbers of MTLBs and other light armor, about sixty tanks, and the capture of over 5,000 POWs. Nearly all the brigade's tanks are still ready for combat, despite the long move and fast pace and the corrosive effect of combat. Of the fifty-nine that launched across the breech, fifty-three are still running on G + 4. Ten 4 Armoured Brigade Rats have been killed in the campaign, another seven wounded. It has been an amazing, incredible experience, and now everyone wants to take a nap.

127

Index